The Gluten-free and Wheat-free

BUMPER BAKE BOOK

This book is the culmination of ten busy years of research to produce special flours and a totally new concept for gluten-free and wheat-free baking and the recipes for their use. It gives a wide selection of baking, attractively presented, so the special dieter may enjoy the variety of food that the rest of us, on just ordinary diets, take for granted.

As always, the author is concerned about special diet food from the nutritional angle as well as taste, appearance and ease of preparation Rita Greer has written seven other books on specialist cookery but this one is the largest and most comprehensive yet for the gluten-free and wheat-free community.

A cookery book for Coeliacs and those with gluten/wheat sensitivity

By the same author:

Introduction to Art and Craft
Introduction to Lettering
Gluten-free Cooking
Diets to Help Multiple Sclerosis
Diets to Help Coeliacs and Wheat Sensitivity
Rita Greer's Extraordinary Kitchen Notebook
Fruit and Vegetables in Particular
The First Clinical Ecology Cookbook
Many Scars and MS Observed
Superb Soups and Starters
Food Allergy — a practical, easy guide
    (with RJ Woodward)

The Gluten~free and Wheat~free BUMPER BAKE BOOK

Rita Greer

Published by Rita Greer, 225 Putney Bridge Road, London SW15 2PY

The publishers apologise for the following slight errors:

Pizza p. 14 add ½ tsp each of cream of tartar and bicarbonate
of soda to the flour.
Vanilla Creams p. 30 add flavouring after the egg.
Ginger Nuts p. 45 add 2 oz (50g) sugar to ingredients.
Butter Biscuits p. 51 heat the sugar with the butter.
Jam Doughnuts p. 90 add the sugar at the same time as the flour.
Bakewell Tart p. 115 add ground almonds with the breadcrumbs.

First published 1982
Second edition 1983
Third edition 1990

© Rita Greer 1982

Illustrations and typesetting by Rita Greer,
Photographs by Stonecastle Graphics,
Tunbridge Wells, Kent. Printed in England
by Errand Press Ltd, 114 Waverley Road,
Southsea, Hants.

ISBN 0 906202 05 1

CONTENTS

INTRODUCTION

The following collection of recipes is suitable for Coeliacs and those with gluten sensitivity (gluten sensitive enteropathies), Dermatitis Herpetiformis and wheat allergy/sensitivity.

All the flours and other ingredients used in this book are naturally free of gluten and wheat. This means that the recipes do not contain wheat, rye, barley or oats in any form. Any ingredients which could possibly have wheat or gluten-containing grains added as a filler during manufacture are marked with a warning star. You will find it used after such items as cocoa*, cornflour* and cooking chocolate*. It indicates that you should check the ingredients box on the appropriate packet.

NUTRITION

As a wide selection of recipes is given it is as well to know which ones offer the best nutritional value. You will find each recipe star rated. The very best ones have five stars and the poorest ones only a single star. The in-betweens have two, three and four stars. Grading depends on several aspects. Stars are deducted for too much fat, salt and sugar and added for good fibre content, vitamin and mineral value, protein value and general nutritional value and not just appearance and taste. Wholefood recipes will naturally rank the highest and no recipe has such a low rating as to have no stars at all. Obviously the five-star recipes should be the ones used most and the one-star recipes are best avoided except on special occasions. Highly processed foods are not used, such as commercial jellies and breakfast cereals.

In an ordinary diet, wheat, rye, barley and oats provide valuable sources of B-group vitamins and cereal fibre. In a wheat-free/gluten-free diet a deficiency of these vitamins may occur, particularly in B1 (Thiamin), B2 (Riboflavin), B3 (Nicotinic Acid), B5 (Pantothenic Acid) and B6 (Pyridoxine). Lack of cereal fibre in the diet can lead to constipation which in turn can lead to other complaints. Both soya bran and rice bran are good substitutes for wheat bran and can be used for a wheat-free/gluten-free diet.

The average diet in the UK leaves much to be desired. We eat far too much fat, sugar and salt. We don't eat enough fresh vegetables and fruit or enough cereal fibre. Most of us eat too much and the result of all these bad eating habits is that our hospital waiting lists are frighteningly long for surgery and treatment that could have been avoided by sensible eating habits. Avoid the queue by balancing your diet in this way:

> 15% fats, oils, nuts and seeds
> 20% meat, fish and eggs
> 45% fresh vegetables and fruit
> 20% special bakery items

Please note the special bakery items form only a small part of the daily diet. And that is the size of the gluten-free/wheat-free problem — a mere one fifth of the diet.

Notes on the special flours and ingredients used in this recipe book
(See back of book for details or suppliers etc.)

1. GROUND RICE — white or brown, not as fine as flour but a useful ingredient.
2. YELLOW SPLIT PEA FLOUR — a bright yellow, finely ground flour with a strong pea taste. Useful in blends as it has a slight ability to bind. Don't use the green variety as it makes baking a dreadful colour!
3. MAIZE FLOUR — finely ground corn-on-the-cob. Not very nutritious with a bland taste. Cornflour (some brands) poses as maize flour sometimes. Cornflour can be any kind of mixture of flours including wheat.
4. SOYA FLOUR — a yellow flour with a good protein content. Don't buy the defatted type by mistake. It has a slightly musty smell and taste but this can be overcome by blending it with other suitable flours.
5. POTATO FLOUR— a fine white starch with a slight potato taste. A poor binder but useful in blends as it will combine well with other flours.
6. TRUFREE and JUBILEE FLOURS — there are 7 altogether, numbered from 1 to 7. Their ingredients vary but are all suitable for wheat free and gluten free diets as they

do not contain wheat in any form or rye, barley or oats.
They are also free of lactose and milk. They are not low
in protein like other gluten free flours but are formulated
to give maximum nutrition .

7. RICE BRAN — made from rice husks, a good substitute for
    wheat bran in a special diet.

8. DRIED PECTIN — an expensive but effective natural binder,
    used in small amounts. Has a slightly metallic taste to
    some people. The dried equivalent of grated apple.

Notes on using the New Trufree/Jubilee Flours

These flours represent an entirely new concept in wheat free/
gluten free baking. They are not like any other flours and so
need their own special recipes.

These recipes are not suitable for use with other gluten free
flours. Similarly, recipes for wheat flour cannot be made with
Trufree/Jubilee flours, although the end products compare
very well and in most cases don't look any different. Recipes
designed for other types of gluten free flours will not work
with Trufree/Jubilee flours.   Use only the flours specified in
the recipes for best results.

Do not use egg replacers with Trufree/Jubilee flours or other
special ingredients as they will not work. The recipes in this
book do not call for any more eggs than would be used in
cooking with wheat flour. Use size 3 eggs unless another size
is indicated in the recipes.

For best results use the lbs and oz measures and not the metric
ones which are put in by law and are rounded up or down. e.g.
very few are really accurate. Always measure and weigh carefully.
Guessing could mean expensive flops.

You will find baking with Trufree/Jubilee flours is not the same
as using wheat flour. Methods are usually quicker, baking times
often shorter and oven temperatures sometimes lower.   Bread
can be prepared in as little as one minute without proving or
kneading as yeast behaves in quite a different way without the

presence of gluten and wheat. Some of the recipes may seem a little bizarre to the experienced cook at first but they will produce appetizing and nourishing food and in the wide variety that we take for granted in the UK.

Do not add baking powder to Trufree/Jubilee No. 6 Plain flour as it will not work in the recipes. The S.R. flour is made to quite a different formula from the Plain. Please note that each number Trufree flour is the same as the corresponding Jubilee flour. e.g. Trufree No. 1 flour is exactly the same as Jubilee No. 1 flour. The reason is that some Trufree flours are on prescription and may not be advertised. Jubilee flours are not on prescription and may be advertised to the public. This is also the reason you will not see Trufree flours on display at the Chemists — this would be classed as advertising too.

Full details of all the Trufree/Jubilee flours can be found in a helpful guide published by the manufacturer. If you would like a free copy please send an SAE to:

**Trufree Foods Dept BB, Larkhall Laboratories,
225 Putney Bridge Road, London SW15 2PY**

Some of the Trufree/Jubilee flours contain wholeground almond. The brown skins are left on the almonds and when they are ground these appear as small specks of brown in the flours.

All the food baked for the photographs in this book was made with Trufree/Jubilee flours under strict supervision and control.

Equipment

You will see that all the equipment is very basic, without any special gadgetry. Non-stick tins are not necessary. Half round shaped patty tins are easier to use than the ones with sloping sides. The old fashioned scales and weights are more accurate than spring scales. For large amounts of cake mix use a washing-up bowl, scrupulously clean. Good, strong equipment which is looked after carefully will last a lifetime.

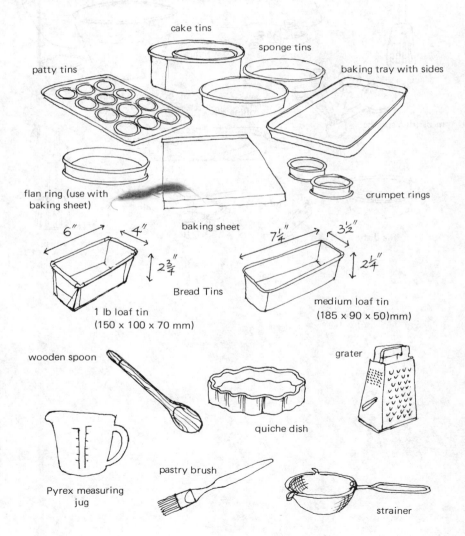

cake tins

sponge tins

patty tins

baking tray with sides

flan ring (use with baking sheet)

crumpet rings

baking sheet

6″   4″   2¾″

Bread Tins

7¼″   3½″   2¼″

1 lb loaf tin
(150 x 100 x 70 mm)

medium loaf tin
(185 x 90 x 50)mm)

wooden spoon

grater

Pyrex measuring jug

quiche dish

pastry brush

strainer

piping bag and nozzles

cutters

spatula

scales and weights

bowls and basins

measuring spoons

rolling pin

pie dish

knife

ramekins

whisk

f

Bread and Scones

NOTES ON YEAST *

The instant yeast used in the bread recipes is marketed under the brand name of Fermipan by several manufacturers who then add their own name. It is labelled 'quick yeast' or 'instant yeast' or 'fast yeast' and should not be confused with dried active yeast or fresh bakers' compressed yeast. Trufree flours Nos. 1,2,3,4 and 5 have ¼ oz sachets (7 g) included in the packs, specially imported from Holland. They are also obtainable by mail order — see details in the back of this book. Always follow instructions in this recipe book and not the ones on the sachets, which are designed for wheat flour bread.

People following a milk free diet should not use Fermipan yeast but dried active yeast or fresh bakers' yeast. Allow the same amount as stated in the recipes for the dried active yeast but double the amount of fresh bakers' yeast. These two yeasts need to be used differently from the Fermipan which is added to the flour dry.

If using dried active yeast, take the liquid in the recipe and crumble in the yeast. Leave to 'work', stir and then add to the flour etc. as directed in the recipe for just the water.

An example of the method for dried active yeast can be seen in the recipe for Jubilee Bread. Needless to say dried active yeast and the fresh bakers' yeast will make the preparation time longer.

Dried active yeast which has been too long on the shelf will usually let you down. Really fresh bakers' yeast is always reliable and used throughout the bakery trade.

Storing Breads: When cold, put into a clean polythene bag and close with a metal tie or a clothes peg. Store in a cool dry place.

Using Bread: Use fresh for sandwiches. Toast or fry in hot oil. Use up stale bread for breadcrumbs and use for coating fish and for Frumble; dry out slices slowly in the oven to make rusks. See Puddings and Pastries Section for Apple Charlotte, Summer Pudding and Fruit on Bread. Make Fisherman's Toast by dipping slices of bread in milk and then in beaten egg. Fry in hot oil on both sides and serve hot. Also make a sweet variation of this by sprinkling with caster sugar.

BASIC WHITE DOUGH — for rolls, croissants, breadsticks,
plaits, French sticks, pizza bases etc.

10 oz Trufree or Jubilee No. 4 white flour (275 g)
¼ oz instant yeast (7 g)
5 fluid oz warm water (150 ml)
1 oz margarine (25 g)
3 pinches salt
1 heaped teaspoon sugar

Preheat oven: Regulo 7 (220°C or 425°F)
Position: top shelf
Baking time: 15 minutes or as indicated in recipes

Method: Put the flour, yeast, salt and sugar into a bowl.
Mix well and add the margarine. Rub in with the fingers. Now
pour in the warm water and mix to a sticky dough. This requires
kneading without adding any more flour. If it turns out too
stiff add another tablespoon warm water. Take out of the bowl
as soon as it makes one ball and knead on a cool worktop. You
should have a smooth and shiny dough after a couple of minutes
kneading. Shape as directed in the following recipes, again
without using more flour. Leave in a warm place to rise. Bake
and take items off trays as soon as they are out of the oven.
Cool on a wire rack. Eat freshly baked and while still warm if
you wish.   This recipe makes about 1 lb of dough (450 g)
suitable for finger rolls and round rolls, croissants, plaits, French
sticks, crisp breadsticks and fancy rolls.   The recipe
should be measured out correctly and not guessed. The following
recipes show how the dough can be used.

FINGER ROLLS

****

Method: Use the Basic White Dough recipe. For each roll use 1 oz dough (25 g). Roll into small sausage shapes and place on a greased baking sheet. Leave to rise in a warm place. When doubled in size bake for 15 minutes. Eat freshly baked.

SESAME ROLLS

****

Method: Use the Basic White Dough recipe. Divide into 12, roll into sausage shapes and coil on a greased baking sheet as shown. Brush with beaten egg and sprinkle with sesame seeds. Leave to double in size in a warm place. Bake for 15 minutes. Eat freshly baked.

TWISTS or KNOTS

****

Method: Use the Basic White Dough recipe. Divide into ½ oz pieces (15 g). Roll into long sausage shapes (thin) and twist carefully as shown. Lay on greased baking sheets and leave to rise in a warm place. Bake for only 10 to 12 minutes. Can be brushed with beaten egg before baking to give a glazed finish but this is optional. Serve with soup or cheese.

Eat freshly baked, preferably still warm from the oven.

BAPS

Method: Use the Basic White Dough recipe.   Use 2 oz of
dough for each bap (50 g). Shape into round flat buns and
leave to double in size on a greased baking sheet, in a warm place.
 Bake for just 10 to 12 minutes and take out of the oven before
they brown. Cool on a wire rack. Use freshly baked for salad rolls
and for hamburgers*.   The baps can also be brushed with beaten
egg and sprinkled with sesame seeds before baking.

****

BREADSTICKS

****

Method: Use the Basic White Dough recipe. Use about ½ oz dough
per bread stick. Roll out into long pencil shapes and put on
to greased baking sheets. When on the baking sheets pinch out
even longer to about 10 inches (25 cms).   Leave to rise in a warm
place — just a few minutes — and bake for 9 or 10 minutes until
golden. Don't worry if you have not rolled them out very neatly
as you will find they will neaten considerably as they rise.   Serve
with soup or instead of rolls with a meal.

FRENCH STICK

****

Method: Make up the Basic White Dough and use half.   Roll out
into a long sausage and put on to a greased baking sheet. Brush
with beaten egg then slash with a sharp knife along the top.
Leave in a warm place to rise and then bake for about 15 minutes
or until golden and crusty. Eat freshly baked.

 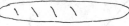 

PLAIT

****

Method: Make up the Basic White Dough and use half. Roll out
into 3 equally sized sausages. Press together at one end, on a
greased baking sheet. Carefully plait and join the ends, shaping
the loaf so that it is widest in the middle. Brush with beaten
egg and sprinkle with poppy seeds (optional). Leave to rise in
a warm place then bake for about 15 to 20 minutes or until
golden brown and crusty. Eat freshly baked.

* Must be gluten-free/wheat-free

MILK ROLLS

****

Method: Use the Basic White Dough recipe but use warm milk that has been scalded and allowed to cool instead of just water. Roll into 12 balls and put on to a greased baking sheet. Leave to double in size, in a warm place. Before baking brush with beaten egg and sprinkle with poppy seeds. Bake for 15 minutes. Eat freshly baked.

CROISSANTS

**

Method: Make the Basic White Dough but add 1 extra teaspoon sugar and increase the salt to ¼ teaspoon (level). For each croissant use 1 oz dough (25 g). On a floured surface* roll out thinly into a square. Over half, as shown, coarsely grate butter, straight from the ice box of the fridge. Just a sprinkle will do. Cut into two, diagonally.

Slip a spatula under the plain half to loosen and fold over on to the buttered half. Seal by pressing round the edges and rolling lightly with a rolling pin. You now have a triangle of pastry. Roll up from the widest edge, very carefully, mending the dough if it cracks. Place on a greased baking sheet, bending each croissant into the traditional crescent shape. Leave to rise until doubled in size. Bake after brushing liberally with beaten egg. They will take about 15 minutes. Serve warm with hot coffee for breakfast or elevenses.

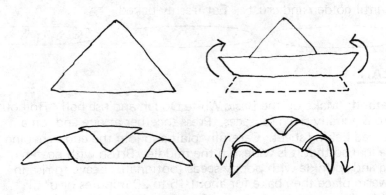

6

* Must be gluten-free/wheat-free

TRUFREE WHITE BREAD — takes only a minute to make and does not require proving or kneading ★★★★

10¼ oz Trufree No. 4 flour (290 g)
¼ oz instant yeast (7 g)
1 tablespoon oil
exactly 8 fluid oz warm water (225 ml)

Preheat oven: Regulo 4 (180°C or 350°F)
Position: top shelf
Baking time: about 1 hour

Method: Put the flour into a bowl. Add the oil and sprinkle in the yeast. Stir. Pour in the water and mix to a creamy batter. Spoon into a greased 1 lb loaf tin and put immediately into the oven to bake. Cool on a wire rack after turning the loaf out of the tin. ❧ **(The special yeast is provided with the flour.)**

TRUFREE BROWN BREAD ★★★★

Method: Use the above instructions for white bread but use Trufree No. 5 flour, which is brown. This loaf will not rise quite as high as the white bread as it has added rice bran. ❧❧❧

TRUFREE FRUIT LOAF ★★★★★

Method: Make up either of the No. 4 or No. 5 flours as directed in Trufree White Bread or Trufree Brown Bread and to the batter add 1 heaped tablespoon dried fruit and 1 level tablespoon sugar. Use currants, sultanas, raisins or mixed fruit. The grated rind of a lemon or an orange can also be used. For variation add a heaped tablespoon chopped walnuts as well. Glaze the top with milk and sugar glaze. (See Glaze for Buns). ❧

TOMATO HERB BREAD ★★★★

Method: Make up Trufree White Bread batter but add 1 heaped tablespoon tomato pureé and 1 level teaspoon oregano (dried). Makes the most amazingly coloured bread. Good for cold meat sandwiches. ❧

MILK LOAF

****

1 teaspoon sugar
10 oz Trufree No. 4 flour
¼ oz instant yeast (7 g) (provided with the flour)
2 oz dried milk granules (50 g)
3 teaspoons oil
8 fluid oz warm water

Preheat oven: Regulo 4 (180°C or 350°F)
Position: top shelf
Baking time: about 1 hour

Method: Put the sugar, flour, yeast and milk granules into a bowl
and mix.❀ Add the oil and water and mix to a creamy batter.
Grease a tin size 7¼ x 3½ x 2¼ inches (185 x 90 x 50 mm).❀
Spoon the mixture into this and put into the oven immediately.
Bake. Turn out on to a wire rack to cool. Cut when cold.
An enriched bread with extra protein from the milk. ❀❀❀

*****

CANTABREAD — a loaf that meets the nutritional requirements
　　　　　　　　of the standard British loaf

10 oz Trufree No. 3 flour for Cantabread (280 g)
3 pinches salt
1 heaped teaspoon sugar
¼ oz instant yeast (7 g) (provided with the flour)
½ pint + 2 tablespoons warm water (310 ml)

Preheat oven: Regulo 5 (190°C or 375°F)
Position: top shelf
Baking time: 1 hour and 10 minutes (approx)

Method: Put the flour into a bowl with the salt, sugar and
yeast. Mix and add the warm water. Stir to a thick batter
and put into a greased loaf tin size 7¼ x 3½ x 2¼ inches
(185 x 90 x 50 mm). Put into the oven immediately and
bake. Turn out of the tin and leave to cool on a wire rack.
Do not cut until cold. ❀

FRUIT CANTABREAD

Method: Make as directed for Cantabread and add 3 oz dried
fruit (75 g) and 1 heaped tablespoon sugar to the batter. ✖

CHEESE AND CELERY BREAD

10 oz Trufree or Jubilee Nos. 4 or 5 flour (275 g)
¼ oz instant yeast (7 g) (provided with the flour)
1 level teaspoon sugar
½ level teaspoon salt
2 level teaspoons celery seeds
2 oz tasty cheddar cheese, grated (50 g)
9 fluid oz warm water (270 ml)

more grated cheese for the top (optional)

Preheat oven: Regulo 4 (180°C or 350°F)
Position: top shelf
Baking time: about 1 hour

Method: Put the flour, yeast, sugar, salt and celery seeds into
a bowl. Mix well. Add the warm water and mix to a batter.
Lastly add the cheese and mix well. ✖ Grease a 1 lb loaf tin
and spoon the batter into this. Sprinkle grated cheese on the
top and bake. Cool on a wire rack. ✖ A really tasty savoury
loaf. ✖

CHEESE AND ONION BREAD

Method: Make as for Cheese and Celery Bread but instead of celery
seeds add a slice of raw onion, put through a garlic press in small
pieces. ✖

GARLIC BREAD

Method: Make as for Trufree White Bread but add one clove of garlic
put through a garlic press. ✍

JUBILEE BREAD (with dried yeast) ****

7 oz Jubilee flour No. 1 (210 g)
¼ teaspoon salt
8 fluid oz warm water (230 ml)
2 slightly heaped teaspoons dried yeast granules
1 tablespoon oil

Preheat oven: Regulo 4 (180° C or 350° F)
Position: top shelf
Baking time: about 1 hour

Method: Measure out the warm water (exactly) and sprinkle
in the yeast. Leave to soften and begin to 'work' for 3 or 4
minutes, with a pinch of sugar if you wish. Put the flour, salt
and oil into a bowl and mix. When the yeast is ready, pour on
to the flour. Mix well and beat to get out any lumps, using a
wooden spoon. Grease and flour* a 1 lb loaf tin. Spoon or
pour the mixture into this and bake immediately until golden
brown and crusty. Turn out on to a wire rack to cool and do
not cut until cold. ♔

This loaf is not only wheat-free, gluten-free and grain-free but
milk-free as well because dried yeast is used and not the instant
type. The flour is the same as Trufree No. 1. Use soya oil or
sunflower oil if baking for a grain allergic and not corn oil or
a mysterious blend of vegetable oils. ♔

BANANA BREAD ****

6 oz Trufree or Jubilee No. 7 S.R. flour (175 g)
2 oz ground rice (50 g)
pinch salt
2 oz margarine (soft) (50 g)
2 oz sugar (soft brown) (50 g)
1 egg, beaten
rind of 1 lemon, finely grated
1 medium-sized banana, mashed

10   * Must be gluten-free/wheat-free

Preheat oven: Regulo 4 (180° C or 350° F)
Position: top shelf
Baking time: 45 to 50 minutes

Method: Put the flour, ground rice and salt into a bowl.   Mix well.
Rub in the margarine with the fingers.   Stir in the sugar, egg, rind and
mashed banana.   Spoon into a greased and floured* small loaf tin.
Bake until light brown. Turn out of the tin and leave to grow cold
on a wire rack. Serve sliced thickly and spread with butter or
margarine. Store in a polythene bag and eat within 2 days.

TRUFREE BREAD (GRAIN—FREE)   ****

7 oz Trufree No. 1 flour (210 g)
¼ level teaspoon salt
8 fluid oz warm water (225 ml)
¼ oz instant yeast (7 g) (provided with the flour)
1 tablespoon oil

Preheat oven: Regulo 4 (180° C or 350° F)
Position: top shelf
Baking time: about 1 hour

Method: Put the flour, salt, oil and yeast into a bowl. Mix well.
Add the water and stir and beat to a smooth batter. Pour into
a greased 1 lb loaf tin and bake immediately. Turn out of the
tin on to a wire rack to cool. Do not cut until cold.   Use an
oil not made from grains such as sunflower or soya oil. The
loaf tin can be floured as well as greased if you wish. Use more
of the Trufree No. 1 flour or potato flour.

* Must be gluten-free/wheat-free

SODA BREAD ***

Just like ordinary Soda Bread made with wheat flour, this is the
poor cousin of bread made with yeast. Eat within a few hours
of baking as it will dry very quickly. Eat cold with plenty of
butter and jam or cheese. Unless baked for a person who is allergic
to yeast use only for emergencies.

8 oz Trufree or Jubilee No. 4 flour (225 g)
1 tablespoon oil
1 teaspoon sugar
¼ pint cold milk (150 ml)
1 heaped teaspoon bicarbonate of soda
1 level teaspoon cream of tartar

Preheat oven: Regulo 7 (220° C or 425° F)
Position: above centre of oven
Baking time: 20 to 30 minutes depending on shape

Method: Put the flour into a bowl with the sugar, bicarbonate of
soda and cream of tartar. Mix really well. Pour in the oil and rub
in. Lastly pour in the milk and mix to a stiff dough. Knead,
using more flour, into a round loaf. Put on to a greased baking
sheet and bake for about 20 minutes. (Cut the top with a knife,
before you bake, into a traditional cross.) Cool on a wire rack.
Alternatively put the dough into a greased 1 lb loaf tin and allow
30 minutes for baking. Take out of the tin when baked and cool
on a wire rack. An ounce of dried fruit can be added to the
flour to make a tea bread (25 g).

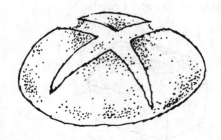

ENRICHED BROWN BREAD WITH RICE BRAN *****

7 oz Trufree or Jubilee No. 2 flour (210 g)
¼ oz instant yeast (7 g) (provided with the flour)
¼ level teaspoon salt
1 tablespoon cooking oil
6 fluid oz warm water (170 ml)
1 egg, beaten

Preheat oven: Regulo 4 (180°C or 350°F)
Position: top shelf
Baking time: 1 hour and 15 minutes

Method: Put the flour, yeast, salt and oil into a bowl. Stir well.
Add the water and mix well. Beat in the egg. Spoon into a greased
1 lb loaf tin and put into the oven immediately. Bake.
Turn out on to a wire rack to cool. Cut when cold. ❀

PIZZA

Two kinds of base can be used for Pizza — a scone dough base
or a bread dough base, which will need to rise before baking.
The same toppings can be used for both kinds of base. Amounts
are given for 1 generous Pizza. See page 14 for toppings.

Pizzas should be crisp on the outside, soft in the middle, and
topped with a variety of savoury toppings and cheese.

BREAD BASE FOR PIZZA ****

Method: Use 3 oz of Basic White Dough (see recipe). Roll
out on a greased baking sheet into a round, flat shape, about
this thickness: .   Brush with oil and cover with
sliced tomato.   Season to taste with salt and freshly
ground black pepper.   Leave to rise in a warm place.
Before baking decorate with one of the suggested toppings.
Bake as for Scone-based Pizza. Serve hot from the oven.

13

Suggested Pizza Toppings

1. Mushroom, sliced and fried in a little oil with a small amount of crushed garlic, sprinkled liberally with cheese.

2. Sprinkle with grated cheese and dot with black olives.

3. Green or red pepper strips, fried in a little oil, sprinkled with grated cheese and a pinch of dried oregano.

4. Sardines, drained of oil, sprinkled with a little cheese and freshly chopped parsley.

5. Diced ham (without breadcrumb coating) and grated cheese, plus 3 or 4 black olives.

SCONE BASE FOR PIZZA   ***

2 oz Trufree or Jubilee No. 4 white flour (50 g)
3 pinches salt
½ oz margarine (15 g)
1½ tablespoons water

Preheat oven: Regulo 7   (220°C or 425°F)
Position: top shelf
Baking time: about 15 minutes

Method: Put the flour into a bowl with the salt and mix.   Rub in the margarine and add the water. Mix and knead to a soft dough, using a little more flour. ❀ Put on to a greased baking sheet and roll or press out to a flat circle about this thick:
Brush with oil and cover with slices of tomato. Season to taste with salt and freshly ground black pepper. Decorate with one of the suggested toppings. Bake and serve still warm from the oven. ❀

PLAIN SCONES — makes 8 ***

4 oz Trufree or Jubilee No. 4 white flour (100 g)
1 level teaspoon bicarbonate of soda
1 level teaspoon cream of tartar
pinch of salt
1 oz soft margarine (25 g)
1 oz sugar (25 g)
exactly 2 tablespoons cold water

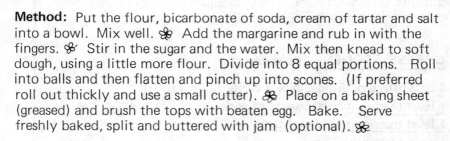

Preheat oven: Regulo 7 (220°C or 425°F)
Position: top shelf
Baking time: 15 minutes

Method: Put the flour, bicarbonate of soda, cream of tartar and salt
into a bowl. Mix well. ❀ Add the margarine and rub in with the
fingers. ❀ Stir in the sugar and the water. Mix then knead to soft
dough, using a little more flour. Divide into 8 equal portions.   Roll
into balls and then flatten and pinch up into scones. (If preferred
roll out thickly and use a small cutter). ❀ Place on a baking sheet
(greased) and brush the tops with beaten egg. Bake.   Serve
freshly baked, split and buttered with jam (optional). ❀

BROWN SCONES ***

Method: Make and bake as for Plain Scones but use Trufree or Jubilee
No. 5 brown flour. ❀

FRUIT SCONES — makes 8 ***

4 oz Trufree or Jubilee No 4 white flour (100 g)
pinch salt
1 oz margarine (25 g)
1 oz sugar (25 g)
1 level teaspoon bicarbonate of soda
1 level teaspoon cream of tartar
1 oz dried mixed fruit (25 g)
exactly 3 tablespoons cold water

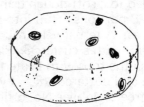

Preheat oven: Regulo 7 (220°C or 425°F)
Position: top shelf
Baking time: 12 to 15 minutes

Method: Put the flour, salt,bicarbonate of soda and cream of tartar
into a bowl. Mix. Add the margarine and rub in with the fingers.
Stir in the sugar, dried fruit and water. Mix, then knead to a soft
dough using a little more flour. 🌸 Divide into 8 equal portions.🌸
Roll into balls, flatten and pinch into scone shapes, or, roll out
and cut into rounds with a small cutter. 🌸 Place on a greased
baking sheet and brush the tops with beaten egg. Bake. 🌸 Eat
freshly baked, split and buttered. 🌸

Variations: Instead of mixed fruit use ONE of the following :—
currants, sultanas, raisins, finely chopped (stoned) prunes, finely
chopped dried apricots. 🌸

CHEESE SCONES — makes 8   ***

4 oz Trufree or Jubilee No. 4 white flour (100 g)

1 level teaspoon bicarbonate of soda

1 level teaspoon cream of tartar

1 oz margarine (25 g)

1 oz grated tasty cheddar cheese (25 g)

exactly 3 tablespoons cold water

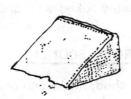

Preheat oven: Regulo 7 (220°C or 425°F)
Position: top shelf
Baking time: 15 minutes

Method: Put the flour, bicarbonate of soda and cream of
tartar into a bowl. Add the margarine and rub in with the
fingers. Stir in the cheese. 🐾 Spoon in the water and mix.🐾
Knead to a soft dough using a little more flour. 🐾 Divide
into 8 portions. Roll into balls, flatten and pinch into scone
shapes. Alternatively, roll out thickly and cut into 8 rounds
(small) with a cutter. 🐾 Place on a greased baking sheet and
brush the tops with beaten egg. Bake. 🐾Serve freshly baked,
split and buttered. 🐾 If you prefer brown scones use
Trufree or Jubilee No. 5 flour. 🐾 Good for snacks as well
as high tea. 🐾

Griddle and Pan Cooking

SINGIN' HINNY — makes 4 triangular scones

****

3½ oz Trufree or Jubilee No. 4 flour (white) (90 g)
1 level teaspoon baking powder*
3 pinches salt
½ oz margarine (15 g)
½ oz caster sugar (15 g)
1 oz currants (25 g)
5 tablespoons milk

Method: Put the griddle or heavy-based frying pan on to heat slowly. 🍀 Mix the flour, baking powder and salt in a bowl. Add the margarine and rub in until the mixture resembles breadcrumbs. 🍀 Stir in the sugar and currants. Make a well in the centre and pour in the milk. Work to make a soft dough. If it is too sticky then add a little more of the flour. Knead on a floured surface and press by hand into a circle about ¼ inch thick (6 mm). 🍀 Grease the griddle or pan. Cut the circle into four quarters and use a spatula to transfer to the griddle or pan. Cook for about 5 minutes on each side, until browned and cooked right through. Serve while still warm, split in half and buttered. 🍀 Serve for a snack or for tea.

Variations:
Use mixed fruit instead of currants plus ½ level teaspoon mixed spice. 🍀

If you would like to make a more wholesome version of this traditional recipe then use Trufree or Jubilee No. 5 flour (brown) and brown sugar. 🍀

* Must be gluten-free/wheat-free

17

CRUMPETS

8 oz Trufree or Jubilee No. 4 flour (225 g)

¼ teaspoon salt

½ teaspoon sugar

¼ oz instant yeast (7 g)

3 teaspoons oil or melted margarine

1 egg

½ pint warm milk (300 ml)

more oil for cooking and greasing

Method: Put the flour, salt, sugar and instant yeast into a bowl and mix. Make a well in the centre. ❦ Put in the 3 teaspoons oil, the egg (beaten) and the warm milk. ★ Mix to a thin batter, then whisk for a few seconds. Leave in a warm place, covered with a clean cloth, to rise and become light and frothy. This will probably take about 30 minutes. When ready, heat a griddle or large heavy-based frying pan. Grease crumpet rings and place on the heat griddle or pan. Into each ring spoon enough of the batter to come two thirds of the way up the ring. Lower the heat. Cook for about 5 minutes, remove the rings and turn the crumpets over to set the tops, for another minute. ❦ Continue until all the batter has been used. Serve right away or, cool on a wire rack and toast on both   sides later. Serve warm with butter.

This recipe makes 12 delicious crumpets. If not used on the day of making they can be frozen for later use. However they are so nice they can be served to the whole family. ❦

If using Dried Active Yeast instead of instant yeast the method of making is slightly different. (Use the same weight of yeast). Put a little of the warm milk into a jug and sprinkle in the dried yeast and sugar. Wait for it to get frothy. Put the flour, salt and 3 teaspoons oil into a bowl and mix. Make a well in the centre and put in the beaten egg, warm milk and the yeast mix. Proceed as from ★ in the previous method.

If using fresh yeast use double the amount of dried yeast. ❦

See the back of this book for details of crumpet rings and where to buy them. You cannot make this recipe without them. ❦

CHAPATIS — to eat with curry   ****

2 heaped tablespoons Trufree or Jubilee No. 7 S.R. flour
pinch salt
3 teaspoons oil
2 tablespoons cold water

Method: Put all ingredients into a bowl and mix to a stiff paste.
Knead, using flour*.   Divide into 4 and roll out thinly using more
flour. Heat a heavy based frying pan or griddle and cook the chapatis
on both sides, without greasing. Stack on a plate until required.
Fry quickly on both sides and serve with curry. They should be
dry and brittle, light and crisp if you have rolled them out thinly
enough.

WELSH CAKES   ****

4 oz Trufree or Jubilee No. 7 S.R. flour (100 g)
2 oz margarine (50 g)
2 pinches salt
½ oz sugar (15 g)
2 oz currants (50 g)
1 egg, beaten
oil for griddle

Method: Rub the margarine into the flour and salt. Stir in the
sugar and the egg. Add currants and mix well. Oil a griddle
or heavy-based frying pan and put over a medium heat. Use a
little more flour to knead the dough and roll it out thickly. Cut
into 10 rounds. Place on the griddle or in the pan and cook for 3
to 4 minutes on each side. Move the cakes around on the surface,
pushing them to the outside edge so that the centres will cook.
Serve warm or cold with butter or margarine.

* Must be gluten-free/wheat-free

PANCAKES — makes 3

2 oz Trufree or Jubilee No. 7 S.R. flour (50 g)
1 egg
¼ pint milk (150 ml)
pinch salt
1 teaspoon caster sugar
oil for frying

Method: Put the flour and egg into a basin and mix/beat to a
stiff paste. ❀ Gradually add the milk and beat to make sure
there are no lumps. ❀ Beat in the salt and sugar. ❀ Heat frying
pan and pour in a little oil. ❀ Pour in one third of the batter,
tilting the pan to cover the base with it.❀ Cook for about two
minutes, loosen with a spatula and toss. ❀ Cook on the other side.
Serve right away with sweet or savoury filling, rolled up on
a warm plate.❀ Repeat with the rest of the batter to make two
more pancakes. If you don't have the courage to toss them, turn
over with a spatula. ❀

LEMON PANCAKES

***

Method: Make Pancakes as above. Sprinkle with fresh lemon
juice and caster sugar. Roll up and sprinkle with more juice and
caster sugar. Serve hot on a warm plate with a spoon and fork. ❀

JAM PANCAKES

**

Method: Make pancakes as above. Spread with jam, sparingly,
and roll up. Sprinkle with caster sugar. ❀

20

ORANGE PANCAKES

***

3 pancakes, freshly made (see Pancake recipe)
1 orange
1 oz granulated sugar (25 g)
1 oz butter (25 g)

Method: Grate the orange finely. Melt the butter in a frying
pan. Add the sugar, orange peel and the juice of the orange. Stir
well while you heat and when it starts to bubble lay a pancake in
the pan and use a spoon to coat it with the mixture. Fold it in half
with a spatula and in half again to make a triangle. Keep warm
while you repeat this with the other two pancakes. Serve right
away.

DROPSCONES — makes about 5

****

4 oz Trufree or Jubilee No. 7 S.R. flour (100 g)
2 pinches salt
1 heaped teaspoon sugar
½ a beaten egg
just over 2½ fluid oz cold milk (75 ml)
oil for griddle

Method: Put the griddle or heavy-based frying pan over a low
heat. Mix flour, salt and sugar in a bowl. Make a well in
the centre and put in the egg. Stir in and gradually add the milk.
Beat to a creamy batter. Oil the griddle or pan. Put the batter
into a jug and pour on to the hot griddle or pan to make flat scones.
Cook until bubbles appear on the surface and the undersides are
brown. Turn with a spatula and cook on the other side. Keep
warm for a few minutes until you serve them by wrapping in a
clean tea towel or napkin. Serve warm with butter or margarine.

POTATO SCONES — makes 4 savoury scones

4 oz mashed potato (100 g)

3 pinches salt

1 generous knob of soft margarine (about ½ oz or 15 g)

2 oz Trufree or Jubilee No. 5 flour (50 g)

1 level teaspoon bicarbonate of soda

Method: Put griddle or heavy based frying pan to heat slowly. Beat the mashed potato with the salt and margarine. Add the flour and bicarbonate of soda. ❦ Mix to a soft dough with a little water if needed. Knead and form into 4 scones about this thickness ⬚. ❦ Grease the griddle or pan and place the scones ⬚ on this. Cook for about 5 minutes on each side, until risen, golden brown and cooked right through. Serve warm, split and buttered. ❦

Note: It is essential to cook these scones slowly so that not just the outside is browned. Eat freshly baked. ❦

SAVOURY POTATO SCONES — makes 4

Method: Make and cook as for Potato Scones but add ONE of the following:—

1. Slice of a medium onion, finely chopped
2. 1 oz cheddar cheese (25 g) finely grated
3. 1 heaped teaspoon finely chopped fresh parsley

Serve split and buttered. Good with home-made soup. Eat freshly made. ❦

Biscuits and Cookies

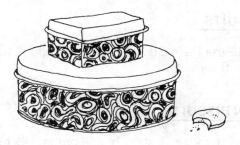

PLAIN BISCUITS — makes about 20 large biscuits

8 oz Trufree or Jubilee No. 7 S.R. flour (225 g)
2 oz soft margarine (50 g)
2 oz sugar (50 g)
1 egg

Preheat oven: Regulo 6 (200°C or 400°F)
Position: top shelf
Baking time: about 15 minutes

Method: Cream the margarine and sugar. ❀ Beat in the egg.
Add the flour and mix to one ball of dough. Knead, using
more of the flour and a little cold water if too stiff. ❀ Roll
out the dough to this thickness ⌷▭⌷ and cut into shapes
with cutters or just divide up with a sharp knife. ❀ Use a
spatula to place on ungreased baking sheets. Prick with a fork
and bake until pale gold. ❀ Cool on a wire rack. Sprinkle
with caster sugar and store in an airtight container. ❀

This is a very useful basic biscuit recipe which can be flavoured,
iced, sandwiched, topped etc. ❀

Easy to make.

COFFEE BISCUITS

Method: Use the Plain Biscuit recipe but add 1 heaped teaspoon of instant coffee* to the flour. ❀ Optional — Ice with white water icing or coffee flavoured water icing when cold. ❀

SPICE BISCUITS

Method: Use the Plain Biscuit recipe but add ½ teaspoon mixed spice* to the flour. ✎

CINNAMON BISCUITS

Method: Use the Plain Biscuit recipe but add ½ teaspoon of cinnamon to the flour. ✿

LEMON BISCUITS

Method: Use the Plain Biscuit recipe but add the finely grated rind of ½ a lemon. Optional — ice with water icing. ✑

ORANGE BISCUITS

Method: Use the Plain Biscuit recipe but add the finely grated rind of 1 orange. 🍊

ICED BISCUITS

Method: Use the Plain Biscuit recipe. Cut into several different shapes with cutters before baking. When baked, leave to grow cold and then ice with different kinds of water icing — coffee, pink, white, yellow etc. (See WATER ICING for instructions). ❀❀❀

* Must be gluten-free/wheat-free

CHOCOLATE BISCUITS

**
Method: Make and bake as for Plain Biscuits but add 1 heaped teaspoon of cocoa (gluten-free and wheat-free) to the flour. If you want to use more cocoa than this use only 7½ oz of the No. 7 flour (215 g) and ½ oz of cocoa (15 g).

TRAFFIC LIGHT BISCUITS   **

Make up the recipe for Plain Biscuits but roll out thinly. Cut into equal sized rectangles. Select half of these and use a thimble or a petit four round cutter to cut out three holes from each, as shown. Bake for about 12 mins at the top of a preheated oven, Regulo 6 (200°C or 400° F). Cool on a wire rack.

When cold, put small blobs of red, orange and green jams on the bottom biscuits. Sandwich with the tops so that the jam shows through the holes.

Very fiddly to make. Don't attempt unless you have plenty of time and patience. Strawberry, apricot and greengage jams are the best for colour. Very popular with children and a novelty at parties!

GINGERBREAD MEN

Method: Make up the Plain Biscuit recipe but add ½ level teaspoon ground ginger to the flour. Roll out and cut into 'men' with a special cutter. Press currants in for eyes and mouth. Bake as for Plain Biscuits.  For a more elaborate finish pipe buttons etc. on to the biscuits with water icing, a fine nozzle and a piping bag.

JAM RINGS

Method: Make up the Plain Biscuit recipe. Cut into rounds and from half of these cut out round centres. Bake the bases and rings as for Plain Biscuits. When cold sprinkle the rings with caster or icing sugar. Spread the bases with jam, varied flavours, and sandwich on the rings.

Very popular with children. Use brightly coloured jams such as raspberry, strawberry, apricot and plum.

BOURBON CREAMS

Traditionally these biscuits are cut into finger shapes. However, it
is very difficult to cut them all the same shape and size. If you don't
do this the resulting biscuits look most odd when they are sandwiched
together. The easiest way round the problem is to use a shaped cutter
such as a half-moon or a small fluted circle.

For the biscuits:
1 oz cocoa* (25 g)
9 oz Trufree or Jubilee No. 6 plain flour (250 g)
pinch salt
4 oz soft margarine (100 g)
4 oz caster sugar (100 g)
1 egg, beaten

For the filling:
3 oz butter (75 g)
5 oz sifted icing sugar (125 g)
1 level teaspoon cocoa*

Preheat oven: Regulo 4 (180°C or 350°F)
Position: centre of oven
Baking time: 20 to 25 minutes

Method: Mix cocoa and flour with salt. Cream margarine and
sugar and gradually add the beaten egg. Put in the dry ingredients
and mix well. Knead until you have one smooth ball of dough.
Roll out thinly and cut out shapes with a cutter. ✳➤ Use a
spatula to place on a greased baking sheet. Bake. Leave to cool
on the baking tray for five minutes and then finish cooling on
a wire rack when the biscuits will go crisp. ✳➤

Put the ingredients for the filling into a basin and beat to a
cream. When the biscuits are cold, sandwich them together
with the filling. Store in an airtight container. ✳➤

As the biscuit dough is very sticky use plenty of the flour for
rolling out, both on the rolling pin and the worktop. Don't
worry if the colour of the flour does not match the biscuit
dough — they will amalgamate during baking. ✳➤

* Must be gluten-free/wheat-free

COFFEE CREAMS

For the biscuits:

1 heaped teaspoon instant coffee*

4½ oz Trufree or Jubilee No.6 plain flour (125 g)

pinch salt

2 oz soft margarine (50 g)

2 oz caster sugar (50 g)

½ beaten egg

For the filling:

1½ oz butter (40 g)

2½ oz sifted icing sugar (60 g)

½ level teaspoon instant coffee*

Preheat oven: Regulo 4 (180° C or 350° F)
Position: centre of oven
Baking time: 20 to 25 minutes

Method: Mix flour and instant coffee with the salt. ❀ Cream margarine and sugar and gradually add the beaten egg. Put in the dry ingredients and mix well. ❀ Knead until you have one smooth ball of dough. ❀ Roll out thinly and cut into similar shapes with a smallish shaped cutter. (Use plenty of flour as the dough can be very sticky.) ❀ Use a spatula to place on a greased baking sheet. Prick with a fork and bake. ❀ Leave to cool on the baking sheet for a few minutes and then transfer to a wire rack to grow cold. ❀ Put the ingredients for the filling into a basin and beat to a cream. When the biscuits are cold, sandwich them together with the filling. Store in an airtight container. ❀

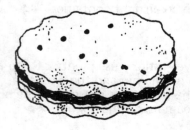

* Must be gluten-free/wheat-free

28

ORANGE CREAMS

For the biscuits:
½ oz cornflour*
4½ oz Trufree or Jubilee No.6 flour, plain (125 g)
pinch salt
2 oz soft margarine (50 g)
2 oz caster sugar (50 g)
½ beaten egg
finely grated rind of ¾ of an orange

For the filling:
1½ oz butter (40 g)
2 ½ oz sifted icing sugar (60 g)
finely grated rind of ¼ of an orange

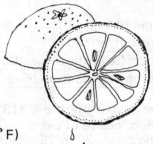

Preheat oven: Regulo 4 (180°C or 350°F)
Position: centre of oven
Baking time: 20 to 25 minutes

Method: Mix flours and salt. ✎Cream margarine and sugar. Add the
beaten egg and grated orange. Add the mixed flours and mix well.
Knead until you have one smooth ball of dough. ✎ Roll out using
more flour and cut into small rounds with a cutter. Use a spatula to
place on a greased baking sheet. ✎ Prick with a fork and bake. ✎
Leave to cool on the baking sheet for a few minutes and then put on
to a wire rack to cool completely. ✎ Put the ingredients for the
filling into a basin and beat to a cream. ✎When the biscuits are cold,
sandwich them together with the filling.   Store in an airtight
container.

LEMON CREAMS

Method: Make and bake as for Orange Creams but use the finely
grated rind of a lemon.✎

* Must be gluten-free/wheat-free

VANILLA CREAMS — makes up to 15 depending on cutter ✱✱

For the biscuits:
4 oz soft margarine (100 g)
4 oz caster sugar
½ a beaten egg
5 oz Trufree or Jubilee No. 6 plain flour (140 g)
about 10 drops vanilla flavouring

For the filling:
1½ oz butter (40 g)
2½ oz sifted icing sugar (60 g)
few drops vanilla flavouring

Preheat oven: Regulo 4 (180°C or 350°F)
Position: centre of oven
Baking time: 20 to 25 minutes

Method: Cream the margarine and sugar. Gradually add the beaten egg. Add the flour and mix well. ✇ Knead into one smooth ball of dough. ✇ Roll out thinly using more of the flour. Cut into shapes with a cutter. ✇ Use a spatula to place the biscuits on a greased baking sheet. Prick with a fork and bake. ✇ Leave to cool on the baking sheet for 5 minutes and then finish cooling on a wire rack when the biscuits will go crisp. ✇   Put the ingredients for the filling into a basin and beat to a cream. When the biscuits are cold, sandwich them together with the filling. ✇ Store in an airtight container. ✇

Optional — Add a pinch of salt to the flour. ✿

WATER BISCUITS — makes about 12 to 15

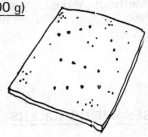

****

4 oz Trufree or Jubilee No. 6 plain flour (100 g)
1 oz soft margarine (25 g)
2 pinches salt
cold water to mix
more flour*for rolling out etc.

Preheat oven: Regulo 8 (230°C or 450° F)
Position: top shelf
Baking time: approx 8 to 10 minutes

Method: Put the flour into a basin with the margarine and salt
and rub in with the fingers until the mixture resembles fine
breadcrumbs. ❀ Add about 1 tablespoon of water and mix to
a stiff paste, using a fork. Add more water if required. ❀
Knead quickly with more flour into one soft lump of dough.
Roll out to this thickness ▭ and cut into squares or
rectangles. ❀ Use a spatula to place them on baking sheets,
(no need to grease them), and prick with a fork. ❀ Bake to
a pale gold colour. Take off the baking sheets and allow to
cool and grow crisp on a wire rack. ❀ Store in an airtight
tin. ❀ Eat as they are or spread with butter or margarine.

Easy to make

COCKTAIL BISCUITS — makes about 50 to 60

****

Method: Make up the Water Biscuit recipe. Roll out and cut into
small biscuits with cutters or a knife. Bake for only 6 to 8
minutes. Serve as party nibbles.

TOMATO BISCUITS

****

Method: Make and bake as for Water Biscuits but instead of using
just water to bind, dissolve 1 heaped teaspoon tomato purée in a
tablespoon water and use this instead. If you need more liquid
top up with water. ❀

* Must be gluten-free/wheat-free

31

CHEESE AND TOMATO BISCUITS

***

Method: Make up the Tomato Biscuits recipe and cut into similar, small shapes. When baked and cold, sandwich together with cream cheese mixed with chopped chives. Eat on day of making. Good for parties.

SESAME CRACKERS

***

Method: Make up the recipe for Water Biscuits. Before baking, brush biscuits with milk and sprinkle with sesame seeds. ❧

CRISPBREADS — makes about 8 large crisp biscuits

****

½ oz rice bran (15 g)
pinch salt
3½ oz Trufree or Jubilee No. 6 plain flour (90 g)
1 oz soft margarine (25 g)
3 tablespoons cold water

Preheat oven: Regulo 8 (230°C or 450°F)
Position: top shelf
Baking time: approx 15 minutes

Method: Put the rice bran into a bowl with the salt and flour. Mix well. Add the margarine and rub in with the fingers until mixture resembles fine breadcrumbs. ❧ Add the cold water and mix into one large lump of dough. Roll out using more flour into a thin sheet of dough. ❧ Use a knife to cut into about 8 rectangles. Lift on to ungreased baking sheets with a spatula and prick all over with a fork. ❧ Bake. Take off the baking sheets with a spatula. Leave to cool and crisp on a wire rack. When cold, store in an airtight container. ❧ If preferred cut into 16 smaller crispbreads. Use instead of bread, spread with butter or margarine etc.

CHEESE WAFER BISCUITS — makes 20 light, crisp biscuits ***

8 oz Trufree or Jubilee No. 6 plain flour (225 g)
2 oz soft margarine (50 g)
3 pinches salt
2 oz finely grated cheddar cheese (50 g)
cold water to mix
more flour for rolling out

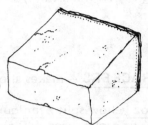

Preheat oven: Regulo 8 (230° C or 450° F)
Position: above centre of oven
Baking time: 20 to 25 minutes

Method: Mix flour and salt in a bowl. Rub in the margarine
until the mixture resembles fine breadcrumbs. 🐟 Stir in
the cheese and mix with a little cold water. Knead into one
large lump of dough. Use more flour to roll out thinly and
cut into about 20 squares or rectangles. 🐟 Use a spatula
to place on to ungreased baking sheets, prick with a fork and
bake until pale gold. 🐟 Leave to get cold on a wire rack —
the biscuits will go crisp as they cool down. 🐟 Store in an
airtight container.

Easy and quick to make. Choose a really tasty cheddar for
best results.

CHEESE NIBBLES ***

Use the recipe above but cut into small biscuit shapes with
little cutters and bake for only 9 or 10 minutes. Allow to cool
on the baking sheets. Serve in a little dish. Ideal for parties.

Makes about 150 miniature biscuits.

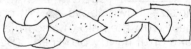

CHEESE AND ONION WAFER BISCUITS ****

Make exactly as for Cheese Wafer Biscuits but before you
sprinkle in the cheese, add a small piece of onion, pressed
through a garlic press. Onion fans will appreciate more
onion than this — add up to four pieces. 🐟

CHEESE AND MARMITE WAFER BISCUITS

Make exactly the same recipe as for Cheese Wafer Biscuits but omit the salt. Before baking, dab the tops of the biscuits lightly with Marmite, using a flat, round-ended knife.

CRACKERS — makes about 16

****

1 oz yellow split pea flour (25 g)
1½ oz ground rice (40 g)
½ oz soya flour (15 g)
½ oz potato flour (15 g)
½ level teaspoon dried apple pectin
1 level teaspoon carob powder
1 heaped teaspoon caster sugar
3 pinches salt
2 teaspoons sunflower oil or similar
2 tablespoons cold water

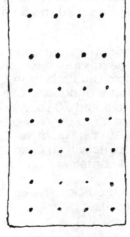

Preheat oven: Regulo 6 (200°C or 400°F)
Position: near top of oven
Baking time: approx 10 minutes

Method: Put all ingredients into a bowl except the water and and rub in the oil as much as you can. Spoon in the cold water and mix with the fingers to a stiff paste until the mixture forms one ball. Using ground rice, roll out to this thickness — ⸤▭⸥. Cut with a knife into rectangular biscuits about the size shown above. Put on to a lightly greased baking sheet with the help of a spatula. Prick all over with a fork and bake until lightly browned. (Be careful not to overbake.) Put on to a wire rack to cool and grow crisp. Store in an airtight container.

Although this recipe sounds an awful lot of trouble to weigh out, the end result is well worth it. If you try them once and really like them, save time on future baking by weighing out a bulk flour mix for the crackers. Store in the fridge in an airtight container and use as required.

FLOUR for CRACKERS (bulk mix)

4 oz yellow split pea flour (100 g)
6 oz ground rice (175 g)
2 oz soya flour (50 g)
2 oz potato flour (50 g)
2 level teaspoons dried apple pectin
1 level tablespoon carob powder
1 slightly heaped tablespoon caster sugar
1 level teaspoon salt

Use 4½ oz of this flour (115 g) with 2 teaspoons of oil and
2 tablespoons cold water. Method is the same as for CRACKERS.

SACRISTANS
***

Method: Roll out pastry more thickly than usual. & Brush with
milk, sprinkle with grated cheese and chopped nuts. Press into the
surface and cut into fingers. Bake as for pastry.

GARIBALDI BISCUITS
***

Method: Use left-over pastry made with Trufree or Jubilee No. 6
plain flour. Roll out and cut in half. Brush one half with milk and
sprinkle with currants and a little sugar. Put the other half of the
pastry on top and go over it with a rolling pin. Cut into fingers or
odd shapes, brush with milk and sprinkle with granulated sugar.
Place on a baking sheet and bake as for pastry in a preheated oven,
Regulo 7 (220°C or 425°F) for about 10 to 12 minutes, top shelf.
Eat freshly baked.

For variation use chopped cooking dates instead of currants.

PEANUT BISCUITS — makes 10

2 oz soft margarine (50 g)
1 oz brown sugar (25 g)
½ beaten egg
2 oz Trufree or Jubilee No.7 S.R.flour (50 g)
3 oz chopped, shelled peanuts (unsalted) (75 g)

Preheat oven: Regulo 4 (180° C or 350° F)
Position: near top of oven
Baking time: approx 15 minutes

Method: Cream the margarine and sugar in a mixing bowl. Add the egg and beat well. 🌿 Fold in the flour and then the nuts. 🌿 Use a teaspoon to place 10 small heaps of the mixture on to a greased baking sheet, leaving plenty of space for the mixture to spread during baking. 🌿 Bake until golden. Leave for a few minutes then lift off with a spatula and finish cooling on a wire rack. Store in an airtight container. 🌿

Other types of nuts can be used instead of peanuts — almonds, walnuts, hazelnuts or a mixture of several kinds. They should be coarsely chopped and not ground. 🌿

ALMONTINES — makes 12 crisp, lacy biscuits

1½ oz butter (40 g)
1½ oz caster sugar (40 g)
2 drops almond flavouring
1 oz Trufree or Jubilee No. 7 S.R. flour (25 g)
1½ oz flaked almonds

Preheat oven: Regulo 6 (200° C or 400° F)
Position: above centre of oven
Baking time: about 20 minutes

Method: Cream the butter and sugar together until light and fluffy. Stir in the almond flavouring, flour and almonds. 🌸 Mix well. Grease baking sheets and place 12 teaspoons of the mixture on them, spaced well apart as they will spread alarmingly. Flatten with damp fingers and bake until pale golden. ❧Take out of the oven but leave on the baking sheets until they begin to set and you can remove them with a spatula or palette knife. Leave to cool and crisp on a wire rack. ❀

CHOCOLATE COVERED BISCUITS — makes about 10 **

1 oz soft margarine (25 g)
1 oz caster sugar (25 g)
½ a beaten egg
few drops vanilla flavouring
4 oz Trufree or Jubilee No. 7 S.R. flour (100 g)
cooking chocolate for covering biscuits*

Preheat oven: Regulo 6 (200°C or 400°F)
Position: top shelf
Baking time: about 15 minutes

Method: Cream the margarine and sugar. ❧ Beat in the egg and the vanilla flavouring. Add the flour and mix to 1 ball. ❧Use more of the flour to knead. (If too stiff add a little cold water.) Roll out to this thickness ⊏━━━⊐ and cut into rectangles, squares and triangles with a sharp knife. ❧ Use a spatula to place on baking sheets — no need to grease them. Bake until golden and cool on a wire rack. ❧ You should be able to make about 10 or 12 biscuits for covering. ❧

Chocolate Covering:

Break about 4 oz (100 g) of cooking chocolate* into small pieces. Put into a bowl over a pan of hot, but not boiling, water. The chocolate will melt gently. When it has all melted, stir to make it thin and free-flowing. Use a knife to spread it on the biscuits, covering the bottoms and sides first and allowing them to set, and finishing with the tops. ❧

* Must be gluten-free/wheat-free

LANGUES DE CHAT — makes up to 30

2 oz butter (50 g)
2 oz caster sugar (50 g)
2 egg whites
2 oz Trufree or Jubilee No. 6 plain flour
vanilla flavouring

Preheat oven: Regulo 6 (200°C or 400°F)
Position: above centre of oven
Baking time: 10 to 12 minutes

Method: Cream the butter and sugar until light and fluffy. Whisk
the egg whites lightly. Gradually add these to the butter/sugar
mixture and beat in. ✿ Fold in the flour and a few drops of the
vanilla flavouring. ✿ Grease and flour baking sheets. ✿ Put the
mixture into a piping bag fitted with a ½ inch (1 cm) plain nozzle
and pipe 3 inch lengths (7.5 cm) of the mixture on to the prepared
baking sheet. ✿ Bake. The biscuits should be a cream colour in
the middle and brown all round the edges. Leave to cool on the
baking sheet for a couple of minutes, then use a spatula to lift off
and transfer to a wire rack to cool and crisp. When quite
cold store in an airtight container. ✿

Use these light, crisp biscuits instead of ice-cream wafers. ✿
Serve with ice-cream, sorbets, fruit fools and fruit salads.

ALMOND BISCUITS — makes about 24

6 oz Trufree or Jubilee No. 7 S.R. flour (175 g)
2 oz ground almonds (50 g)
2 oz soft margarine (50 g)
2 oz soft brown sugar (50 g)
1 egg
few drops almond flavouring

Preheat oven: Regulo 6 (200° C or 400° F)
Position: top shelf
Baking time: about 15 minutes

Method: Mix the flour with the ground almonds. 🌸 Cream the margarine and sugar. Beat in the egg and flavouring. 🌸 Add the flour mixture and mix to one ball, using more of the flour and a little cold water or milk if the dough is too dry. Roll out to this thickness ⬜ and cut into fingers with a sharp knife. Place on baking sheets which are well greased, using a spatula. 🌸 Prick with a fork and bake until golden but not browned. 🌸 Cool on a wire rack and store in an airtight container.

**

LINZER BISCUITS — makes about 10 to 12

8 oz Trufree or Jubilee No. 7 S.R. flour (225 g)
2 pinches cinnamon
2 pinches ground cloves
2 oz soft margarine (50 g)
2 oz caster sugar (50 g)
1 egg
blackcurrant or raspberry jam
icing sugar

Preheat oven: Regulo 6 (200° C or 400° C)
Position: top shelf
Baking time: about 12 minutes

Method: Mix the flour and spices. 🌿 Cream the margarine and sugar. Beat in the egg. 🌿 Add the flour and mix to one ball of dough. Knead, using more of the flour and a little cold water if too stiff. 🌿 Roll out the dough to this thickness ⬜ and cut into rounds with a medium fluted cutter. Cut a hole in the centre of half of the rounds with a clover-leaf petit four cutter or a thimble. 🌿 Use a spatula to place on ungreased baking sheets. Prick lightly with a fork and bake until pale gold. Cool on a wire rack. 🌿 When cold, spread the bases with ½ teaspoon jam. Dredge the tops with icing sugar and press on to the bottoms so that the jam shows through the holes. Store in an airtight container. 🌿

CHOCOLATE CHIP BISCUITS — makes about 20

4 oz soft margarine (100 g)

2 oz brown sugar (50 g)

1 egg beaten

4 oz Trufree or Jubilee No. 7 S.R. flour (100 g)

6 oz chocolate chips for cooking* (175 g)

Preheat oven: Regulo 4 (180° C or 350° F)
Position: near top of oven
Baking time: about 15 minutes

Method: Cream the margarine and sugar in a mixing bowl.
Add the egg and beat well. Fold in the flour and then the
chocolate chips. ❀ Use a teaspoon to place small heaps of
the mixture on to greased baking sheets, leaving plenty of
space for the biscuits to spread during baking.❀ Bake until
golden and leave on the baking sheets for a minute or two.
Lift off with a spatula and finish cooling on a wire rack.
Store in an airtight container. ❀

Half Recipe — for 10 biscuits (use same method)

2 oz soft margarine (50 g)

1 oz brown sugar (25 g)

½ a beaten egg

2 oz Trufree or Jubilee No. 7 S.R. flour (50 g)

3 oz chocolate chips for cooking* (75 g)

* Must be gluten-free/wheat-free

CRISP BISCUITS — makes about 12 egg-free and milk-free biscuits

****

3 level tablespoons yellow split pea flour
2 heaped tablespoons ground rice
1 slightly heaped tablespoon soya flour
½ level teaspoon dried pectin
1 heaped teaspoon carob powder
3 heaped teaspoons caster sugar
pinch salt
2 teaspoons sunflower or soya oil
flavouring from list below
2 tablespoons cold water

Preheat oven: Regulo 6 (200°C or 400°F)
Position: top shelf
Baking time: 8 to 10 minutes

Method: Combine all the ingredients, except the water, in a
small bowl. Rub in the oil with the fingers. Pour in the water
and mix to a sticky paste. Knead to form one ball.   Roll out
to this thickness ⊏━━━⊐ using more ground rice. ✺ Cut into
squares and lift on to an oiled baking sheet, using a spatula. ✺
Prick with a fork. ✺ Bake, being careful not to let them brown
too much. Put on to a wire rack to cool and grow crisp. Sprinkle
with caster sugar. Store in an airtight container. ✺

Select ONE flavouring from this list:

½ level teaspoon ground ginger
¼ level teaspoon powdered cloves (or less)
¾ level teaspoon mixed spice*
¾ level teaspoon cinnamon
1 extra heaped teaspoon carob powder

* Must be gluten-free/wheat-free

41

ALMOND GALETTES

— makes 24 light biscuits with an attractive, munchy topping.

For the biscuits:

4 oz soft margarine (100 g)

2 oz caster sugar (50 g)

1 egg yolk

2 oz ground almonds (50 g)

few drops almond flavouring

6 oz Trufree or Jubilee No. 6 plain flour (175 g)

For the topping:

4 oz icing sugar, sifted (100 g)

1 egg white

2 oz shredded almonds (50 g)

Preheat oven: Regulo 4 (180° C or 350° F)
Position: near top of oven
Baking time: 15 to 20 minutes

Method: To make the biscuit bases, cream the margarine and sugar by beating well. Add the egg yolk and beat again. ❀ Put in the ground almonds, flour and almond flavouring and mix well. ❀ Roll out thinly using more flour. ❀ Cut into rounds using a 2½ inch round cutter with a fluted edge (6 cm). Use a spatula to place on greased baking sheets. ❀

To make the topping, mix the egg white and icing sugar, then add the shredded almonds. ❀Stir well and use a teaspoon to spoon on to the biscuits. Just make a blob of the mixture in the centre of each biscuit and it will spread on its own during baking. ❀ Bake until golden. Cool on the baking sheets and when cold remove with a spatula. Eat on the day they are baked.❀

Although easy to make, these biscuits are quite spectacular. The whole family will love them. ❀

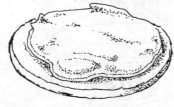

DIGESTIVES — makes 12

2 oz Trufree or Jubilee No. 7 S.R. flour (50 g)
2 oz Trufree or Jubilee No. 6 plain flour (50 g)
1 level tablespoon rice bran
pinch salt
1 small pinch powdered cloves
1 oz soft margarine (25 g)
1 oz soft brown sugar (25 g)
5 or 6 drops fresh lemon juice
½ beaten egg

Preheat oven: Regulo 6 (200° C or 400° F)
Position: above centre
Baking time: 12 to 15 minutes

Method: Put the flours, bran, salt and powdered cloves into
a basin. Mix well. ✳️Add the margarine and rub in. ✳️✳️
Stir in the sugar and lemon juice. Mix in the egg and a
little more of the No. 6 flour so that you can knead the
mixture into one ball of smooth dough.✳️ Roll out to this
thickness ⊏═══⊐ and cut into rounds. Place on greased
baking sheets and prick with a skewer or fork. ✳️ Bake until
light brown.✳️Cool on a wire rack and store, when cold, in
an airtight container. ✳️

N.B. In ordinary baking the flavour of digestive biscuits is made by
wholewheat (brown) flour and oatmeal. As neither of these can be used
in gluten-free and wheat-free cooking cloves and lemon juice are added
for a subtle flavour. The pinch of powdered cloves should be minimal
or the biscuits will be too spicy.

CHOCOLATE DIGESTIVES — makes 12

Method: Make and bake the Digestive Biscuits as above.   When
cold spread on one side with a layer of melted cooking chocolate*
and leave to set on a wire rack. Store in an airtight container.

CHOCOLATE ORANGE DIGESTIVES — makes 12

Method: Use the recipe for Digestive Biscuits but omit the cloves
and lemon juice. Instead, add the finely grated rind of 1 orange.
Top with chocolate as for Chocolate Digestives.

* Must be gluten-free/wheat-free

GINGER THINS — makes 12 light, crisp biscuits

1 oz soft margarine (25 g)
2 level tablespoons golden syrup
1 oz brown sugar (25 g)
3 oz Trufree or Jubilee No. 7 S.R. flour
½ level teaspoon ground ginger

Preheat oven: Regulo 5 (190°C or 375° F)
Position: above centre of oven
Baking time: approx. 10 minutes

Method: Melt the margarine, syrup and sugar in a saucepan.
Cool for 2 minutes and then sift in the flour and ginger. Mix.
Grease baking sheets well. Put teaspoonfuls of the mixture
on to the baking sheets, placing them well apart so they have
room to spread. ✿ Flatten slightly and bake until brown.
Leave on the baking sheets for a minute and then lift off
very carefully with a spatula. ✿ Cool on a wire rack.
Store in an airtight container.

When the biscuits are just cooked they will be soft. As they
cool down so they will grow crisp. Be careful not to overbake. ✿

DARK GINGER THINS ✿

Use the recipe above for Ginger Thins but use black treacle
instead of golden syrup.

SPICE THINS

Use the Ginger Thins recipe but leave out the ginger. Instead,
use ½ level teaspoon ground mixed spice *. ✿

CINNAMON THINS

Use the recipe for Ginger Thins but use cinnamon instead of
ground ginger — ½ level teaspoon. ✿

44

* Must be gluten-free/wheat-free

GINGER NUTS — makes about 15 or 16   **

4 oz Trufree or Jubilee No. 7 S.R. flour (100 g)
1 level teaspoon dried ginger
3 pinches powdered cloves
1 oz soft margarine (25 g)
½ a beaten egg
2 tablespoons golden syrup

Preheat oven: Regulo 4 (180°C or 350°F)
Position: above centre of oven
Baking time: 12 to 15 minutes

Method: Put the flour, ginger and ground cloves into a basin
and mix well. ✂ Beat the margarine to a light cream. Add
the sugar and beat again. Next, beat in the egg and syrup.
✂ Add the dry ingredients and mix to a very stiff paste.
Knead, using more flour, and roll between your palms into
about 16 balls. ✂ Put on to greased baking sheets and flatten
out to about this size:—

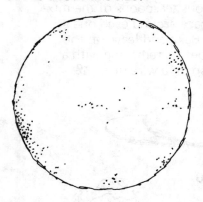

Bake and put on to a wire
rack to cool. Sprinkle with
a little caster sugar. Store in
an airtight container. ✿

DARK GINGER NUTS   **

Use the same recipe as for Ginger Nuts but use 1 tablespoon of
golden syrup and 1 tablespoon black treacle. Real fans of black
treacle will like all black treacle and no golden syrup. ✂
Warm the treacle slightly before measuring to make it easier. ✂

GINGER CRISPS — makes 18 to 20 biscuits

3 oz Trufree or Jubilee S.R. No. 7 flour (75 g)

1 teaspoon (level) dried ginger

3 pinches powdered cloves

1½ oz soft margarine (40 g)

1½ oz caster sugar (40 g)

½ an egg, beaten

3 tablespoons golden syrup

Preheat oven: Regulo 4 (180°C or 350°F)
Position: above centre of oven
Baking time: 12 to 15 minutes

Method: Put the flour, ginger and cloves into a basin and mix
well. ❧ Cream the margarine and sugar. Add the syrup and
cream again. Put in the egg and beat well. ❧ Now tip in the
dry ingredients mixture and stir to a creamy consistency. ❧
Grease baking sheets and drop generous teaspoons of the mixture on to them, leaving plenty of space around each one as
these biscuits spread alarmingly. ❧ Bake and leave on the
baking sheets to cool for 5 minutes before removing with a
spatula. ❧ Put to cool and grow crisp on a wire rack. ❧
Store in an airtight container. ❧

BRANDY SNAPS — makes about 10

1 oz caster sugar (25 g)

1 oz margarine (25 g)

1 level tablespoon syrup

2 oz Trufree or Jubilee No. 7 S.R. flour (50 g)

¼ level teaspoon ginger

Preheat oven: Regulo 3 (160°C or 325°F)
Position: middle shelf
Baking time: 8 to 10 minutes

46

Method: Put the sugar, margarine and syrup into a small sauce-pan and heat gently until the margarine has melted. Mix ginger with the flour. ❀ Stir in well to make a thick, smooth batter in the saucepan. ❀ Liberally grease a baking sheet. Drop teaspoons of the batter on to it, leaving plenty of space around each one to allow for spreading. ❀ Bake until golden brown and bubbly. Take out of the oven and allow to cool for a minute. Loosen with a spatula, one by one, and roll around the handle of a wooden spoon. Leave to crisp on a wire rack. (If they crisp too quickly for this, put back in the oven for a few seconds to soften again.) Store in an airtight container on their own and not with other items. ❀

Serve just as they are or with whipped cream at each end for parties.

***

BOUDOIR FINGERS — makes about 20 delicate biscuits

2 oz caster sugar (50 g)

2 eggs

vanilla flavouring (optional)

3 oz Trufree or Jubilee No. 6 plain flour (75 g)

caster sugar for sprinkling

Preheat oven: Regulo 5 (190° C or 375° F)
Position: above centre of oven
Baking time: 6 to 8 minutes

Method: Put a mixing bowl over a pan of hot water. Put in the sugar, eggs and a few drops vanilla flavouring. ❀ Whisk with a hand whisk until thick. (If you are lucky enough to have an electric beater you won't need the pan of hot water.) ❀ Fold in the flour. Liberally grease and flour baking sheets.   Either do it the lazy way and save on washing up by spooning into narrow finger shapes or, put the mixture into a piping bag fitted with a ½ inch plain nozzle (1 cm) and pipe into finger lengths. ❀ Sprinkle generously with caster sugar and bake until golden. Immediately they are baked, take off the baking sheets with a spatula and cool on a wire rack. ❀ When cold store in an airtight tin. ❀

Can be served with ice cream or fruit fool. ❀

RICH SHORTBREAD — makes about 30   **

3 oz butter (75 g)

2 oz caster sugar (50 g)

½ a beaten egg

7 oz Trufree or Jubilee No. 7 S.R. flour (200 g)

2 pinches salt

cold water

Preheat oven: Regulo 4 (180° C or 350° F)
Position: centre of oven
Baking time: about 20 minutes

Method: Cream butter and sugar. Add the egg and mix well.
Sprinkle in the flour and salt. Use a wooden spoon to mix to
a stiff paste, adding a little cold water if required. ❀❥ Use
more of the flour to knead into 1 ball of dough. Roll out to
this thickness ⌸ and cut into about 30 biscuits, this size.

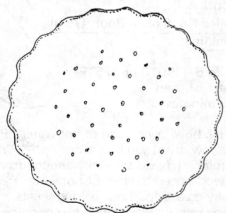

Use a spatula to place on ungreased baking sheets. Prick with
a fork or skewer and bake until pale gold. Sprinkle with
caster sugar if you wish and cool on a wire rack. When cold
store in an airtight container. ❀❥

If you let these brown during baking they will become over-
baked and dry. They should still be a creamy colour when
they are ready to come out of the oven. ❀❥

48

VIENNESE FANCIES

4 fluid oz thin cooking oil (120 ml)
2½ oz icing sugar, sifted (65 g)
finely grated rind of 1 orange
6 oz Trufree or Jubilee No. 6 plain flour (175 g)
2 oz maize flour or cornflour* (50 g)

apricot jam
cooking chocolate*

Preheat oven: Regulo 4 (180°C or 350°F)
Position: above centre of oven
Baking time: about 20 minutes

Method: Put the oil, icing sugar and orange rind into a bowl and
stir well. Put in both flours and mix well.   Grease and flour* baking
sheets using more of the No. 6 flour. Use a piping bag fitted with
a 1 inch fluted nozzle (2.5 cm) and pipe 'fingers' on the prepared
baking sheets. Make them all the same length — about 3 inches or
(7.5 cm), and leave space between them. Bake. Remove from baking
sheets with a spatula and cool on a wire rack. When cold, sandwich
together with apricot jam. Melt the chocolate in a small bowl, over
a pan of hot water. Dip both ends of the sandwiched fingers
in the melted chocolate and leave to set on greaseproof paper.
You will need not less than 3 oz (75 g) of the chocolate and plain
is best. This recipe should produce about 10 double biscuits.

Variation: Make the shortbreads with a few drops of vanilla
flavouring instead of the orange rind. When baked and cooled,
sandwich together with raspberry jam. Dust with icing sugar.
If preferred these can be piped into round whirls instead of
finger shapes. Serve in cake papers because of the icing sugar.

Store in an airtight container but eat up fairly quickly.

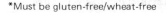

*Must be gluten-free/wheat-free

RICH SHORTCAKES — makes 10

2 oz butter (50 g)
1½ oz icing sugar (40 g)
1 oz cornflour*
3 oz Trufree or Jubilee No.6 plain flour (75 g)

Preheat oven: Regulo 4 (180° C or 350° F)
Position: centre of oven
Baking time: about 15 minutes

Method: Cream the butter and icing sugar well. Add the flours and mix to a stiff paste.   Divide the paste into 10 equal portions. Roll these into balls and flatten between the palms. Place on a greased baking sheet, well spaced out so they can spread. Bake but do not let them brown. Leave to cool on the baking sheet for a few minutes. Lift off carefully with a spatula and allow to grow cold on a wire rack. Store in an airtight container.

ORANGE SHORTCAKES

Method: Use the Rich Shortcake recipe but add the finely grated rind of one orange to the creamed butter and icing sugar.

LEMON SHORTCAKES

Method: Use the Rich Shortcake recipe but add the finely grated rind of ½ a lemon to the creamed butter and icing sugar.

BUTTER BISCUITS — makes about 15 delicious, light biscuits

2 oz butter (50 g)
2 oz soft brown sugar (50 g)
½ a beaten egg
3 oz Trufree or Jubilee No. 7 S.R. flour (75 g)
15 split almonds for decoration (optional)

50

* Must be gluten-free/wheat-free

Preheat oven: Regulo 4 (180°C or 350°F)
Position: centre of oven
Baking time: 12 to 15 minutes

Method: Put the butter into a medium sized saucepan, over a gentle heat and melt. (Do not let it brown). Remove from heat and allow to cool for a minute or two. Beat in the egg and flour. Grease 2 baking sheets and drop teaspoonfuls of the mixture on to it, well apart to allow for spreading. Put a split almond into the centre of each one and bake until golden and browning around the edges. Take off the baking sheets with a spatula and put on to wire racks to crisp and grow cold. Best eaten freshly baked but can be stored in an airtight container.

JAM COOKIES — makes about 15   ***

1 oz shelled almonds, coarsely ground (25 g)
2 oz soft margarine (50 g)
3 oz soft brown sugar (75 g)
½ a beaten egg
3 drops almond flavouring
4½ oz Trufree or Jubilee No. 7 S.R. flour (115 g)
2 tablespoons apricot jam

Preheat oven: Regulo 5 (190°C or 375°F)
Position: above centre
Baking time: about 20 minutes

Method: Cream the margarine and sugar until light. Beat in the egg and almond flavouring. Stir in the flour to make a smooth paste. Use both hands to shape the mixture into balls. Roll these in the ground almonds and place on a well-greased baking sheet, spaced well apart as the cookies will spread. Use your thumb to make a deep dent in the centre of each ball. Fill these dents with apricot jam, using a teaspoon. Bake. Leave on the baking sheet for 5 minutes then transfer to a wire rack to cool completely. Store in an airtight container.

Don't be tempted to be too generous with the jam or it will bubble out over the cookies. For variety use other flavours of jam such as raspberry and strawberry.

BABY RUSKS — makes about 14 dry biscuits

1 oz Marvel dried milk (25 g)
3 oz Trufree or Jubilee No. 7 S.R. flour (75 g)
2 oz soft margarine
2 oz soft brown sugar
½ a beaten egg

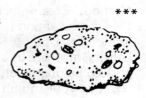

Preheat oven: Regulo 6 (200° C or 400° F)
Position: above centre of oven
Baking time: about 10 minutes

Method: Mix the dried milk with the flour. Cream the
margarine and sugar. Beat in the egg. Add the flour mix
and a little cold water if the dough is too dry. Knead into 1
ball of soft dough. Divide into 14 and roll into balls. Place
on a greased baking sheet and flatten with your palm. Press
a fork into the top of each one to make a ridged pattern.
Bake until golden but not too browned. Cool on a wire rack.
Store in an airtight container.

Crumble into milk to make a cereal type meal. The taste is
rather bland, suitable for babies. The sugar can be cut to
1 oz if desired (25 g). Each biscuit contains about 2 g of
protein.

COOKIES (Rice-based) — makes 4 or 5 cookies   ***

1 oz soft margarine (25 g)
2 oz ground rice (50 g)
1 oz sugar (25 g)
1½ oz finely grated eating apple (40 g)

fruit, nuts, spices, flavouring etc of choice (see variations)

Preheat oven: Regulo 8 (230° C or 450° F)
Position: above centre of oven
Baking time: 20 to 25 minutes

52

Method: Put the margarine and ground rice into a bowl and blend with a fork. Add the remaining ingredients including the flavouring etc. of your choice and knead into 1 ball. ✿ Grease a baking sheet and drop the dough on to it in 4 or 5 heaps, leaving plenty of space around them. ✿ Spread into cookie shapes with a knife, about this thick ▭. Bake until browning slightly. Allow to cool on the baking sheet for a couple of minutes and then remove with a spatula. ✿ Finish cooling on a wire rack or eat warm, sprinkled with a little caster sugar if you wish. Eat the same day.

WHOLEFOOD COOKIES ****

To make this recipe into a wholefood one, use wholeground brown rice and soft muscovado sugar. Grate the apple with the skin left on. Omit sprinkle of sugar at the end.

Here are 6 variations using this basic recipe.

CHOCOLATE NUT COOKIES ***

Method: Use the basic Cookies recipe. Add 1 level teaspoon of cocoa* and press half a walnut into the top of each cookie. ✿

CURRANT COOKIES ***

Method: Use the basic Cookies recipe. Add the finely grated rind of ½ a lemon and ½ oz currants (15 g). ✿

PRUNE COOKIES ***

Method: Use the basic Cookies recipe and add the finely grated rind of ½ a lemon. Remove the stones from 3 or 4 prunes and discard. Chop the prunes and add to the dough. ✿

APRICOT COOKIES ***

Method: Use the basic Cookies recipe. Add ¼ teaspoon cinnamon and 1 oz dried apricots (25 g) chopped small. ✿

* Must be gluten-free/wheat-free

DATE COOKIES

***

Method: Use the basic Cookies recipe. Add the finely grated rind of ½ a medium orange and about 1 oz (25 g) cooking dates, chopped small. ✻

SULTANA COOKIES

***

Method: Use the basic Cookies recipe. Add ½ oz sultanas (15 g) with the rind of half an orange, finely grated. ✻

HONEY COOKIES — makes 16 rich cookies

**

2 oz butter (50 g)
2 oz brown sugar (50 g)
½ a beaten egg
few drops vanilla flavouring
4 oz Trufree or Jubilee No. 7 S.R. flour (100 g)
1 oz maize flour or cornflour*
1 level tablespoon runny honey

Preheat oven: Regulo 4 (180°C or 350°F)
Position: above centre of oven
Baking time: about 15 minutes

Method: Cream the butter and sugar until light and fluffy. Add the egg and vanilla flavouring and mix well. Put in the flours and mix again. Finally, put in the honey and mix again to a smooth paste. Roll into 16 balls. ✻ Put on to a greased baking sheet and flatten slightly. (Leave plenty of space around each one as they will spread during baking.) Bake until dark golden. ✻ Leave on the baking sheet for few minutes before you take them off with a spatula. ✻ Cool on a wire rack. Store in an airtight container. ✻

To make less rich cookies use margarine instead of butter. ✻

54   * Must be gluten-free/wheat-free

MUESLI COOKIES — makes 20 light, speckled cookies

4 oz soft margarine (100 g)
1 oz brown sugar (25 g)
3 generous teaspoons runny honey
1 egg
4 oz Trufree or Jubilee No.7 S.R. flour (100 g)
2 heaped teaspoons sunflower seeds
2 heaped teaspoons sesame seeds
3 oz chopped mixed nuts (75 g)
2 oz raisins (50 g)

Preheat oven: Regulo 4 (180° C or 350° F)
Position: near top of oven
Baking time: 15 minutes

Method: Put the margarine, sugar, honey, egg and flour into a
mixing bowl. ✿ Mix and beat to a creamy consistency. Add the
remaining ingredients and mix in. ✿ Grease baking sheets and
place small heaps of the mixture on these, leaving plenty of room
for the cookies to spread during baking. ✿ Bake until golden
brown round the edges. Leave to cool on the baking sheets for a
few minutes. ✿ Transfer to a wire rack to cool, using a spatula.

Best eaten freshly baked but will keep in an airtight container.✿
For the nut mixture use almonds, walnuts, hazelnuts and peanuts.

Half recipe — makes 10

2 oz soft margarine (50 g)
1 heaped teaspoon brown sugar
2 teaspoons runny honey
½ a beaten egg
2 oz Trufree or Jubilee No. 7 S.R. flour (50 g)
1 heaped teaspoon each of sunflower and sesame seeds
1½ oz mixed chopped nuts (40 g)
1 oz raisins (25 g)

MACAROONS   ***

These moist cookies keep extremely well and are easy to make. They
are ideal for packed meals as they won't break in transit. Grind your
own shelled nuts in an electric coffee grinder — there is no need to
blanch them.

ALMOND MACAROONS — makes about 12   ***

4 oz caster sugar (100 g)
2½ oz ground almonds (75 g)
2 level teaspoons ground rice
2 egg whites
rice paper
12 split almonds or 6 halved glacé cherries

Preheat oven: Regulo 4 (180° C or 350° F)
Position: above centre of oven
Baking time: approx. 20 minutes

Method: Put the sugar, ground nuts and ground rice into a
bowl. Mix well. ✿ Put the egg whites into a small bowl and
whisk lightly until they begin to stiffen. ✿ Add the dry
ingredients from the first bowl and mix well. The mixture
should be shiny and smooth. ✿ Line a baking sheet with
rice paper. Use a teaspoon to divide the mixture into 12
amounts and put them on the rice paper, leaving plenty of
space between them as they will spread during baking.   Press
a split almond or half-cherry into the middle of each one.
Bake until golden and leave to cool on the baking sheet. ✿
When cold, trim off excess rice paper with kitchen scissors.
Store in an airtight container. ✿

If you want to make a larger quantity, here is a double ingredient list.
Method is the same but make into 24 instead of 12 macaroons.

Double recipe

8 oz caster sugar (225 g)
5 oz ground almonds (150 g)
1 level tablespoon ground rice
4 egg whites
rice paper
24 split almonds or 12 halved glacé cherries

RATAFIAS

These are made exactly like
Almond Macaroons
without the nut decoration
and very much smaller. Each
Macaroon will make into 6
Ratafias. Shorten the baking
time by 5 minutes. Use to
decorate Trifles.

HAZELNUT MACAROONS — makes 12

4 oz soft brown sugar (100 g)
2½ oz ground hazelnuts (75 g)
2 level teaspoons ground rice
2 egg whites
12 whole hazelnuts for decoration

Method: Make and bake in the same way as Almond Macaroons.

MIXED NUT MACAROONS — makes 12

4 oz soft brown sugar (100 g)
2½ oz mixed, ground nuts — choose from almonds,
  hazelnuts walnuts, unsalted peanuts — (75 g)
2 level teaspoons ground rice
2 egg whites
6 glacé cherries, halved for decoration

Method: Make and bake in the same way as Almond Macaroons.

COFFEE and WALNUT MACAROONS — makes 12

4 oz soft brown sugar (100 g)
2½ oz ground walnuts (75 g)
2 level teaspoons ground rice
2 egg whites
1 heaped teaspoon instant coffee (or less)
12 pieces walnut for decoration

Method: Make and bake in the same way as Almond Macaroons
but add the instant coffee (use a gluten-free, wheat-free brand)
to the bowl of dry ingredients.

NUT CRUNCHIES — makes 12 small ones   ***

4 oz caster sugar (100 g)
2½ oz ground almonds or hazelnuts (75 g)
2 level teaspoons ground rice
1 egg white
rice paper

Preheat oven: Regulo 4 (180°C or 350°F)
Position: centre of oven
Baking time: approx 25 minutes

Method: Put the sugar, ground nuts and ground rice into
a bowl. Mix well. Put the egg white into a large cup and
whisk until it stiffens. Add to the dry ingredients and mix to
a dryish paste. Line a baking sheet with rice paper. Divide
the paste into 12 and roll into balls. Place on the rice paper
and press to flatten. Bake until light brown. Leave to cool
on the baking sheet. When cold trim off excess rice paper
with kitchen scissors.

Optional — Decorate each one with a split almond.

Can be stored for several weeks in an airtight container.

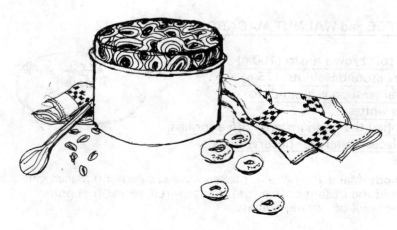

Cakes

APPLE CAKE

****

2 oz soft margarine (50 g)

2 oz soft brown sugar (50 g)

1 egg

4 oz Trufree or Jubilee No. 7 S.R. flour (100 g)

1 level teaspoon cinnamon or ½ teaspoon mixed spice

2 oz coarsely grated cooking apple (50 g)

granulated sugar for top

Preheat oven: Regulo 5 (190°C or 375°F)
Position: above centre
Baking time: about 1 hour

Method: Grease and flour a small loaf tin (traditional 1 lb size). Put the first five ingredients into a mixing bowl and mix/beat to a soft consistency. Add the apple and mix again. Spoon into the prepared tin and bake, sprinkling with the granulated sugar before you put it into the oven. Bake, turning down the heat to Regulo 4 (180°C or 350°F) after 30 minutes. Continue on this heat for the last 30 minutes. Allow to cool in the tin for five minutes before turning out to cool on a wire rack. Eat within 48 hours of baking. Store in an airtight container, in the fridge. A soft, moist cake.

Variation: add a sprinkle of sultanas to the mix.

59

RICH CHOCOLATE CAKE   *

7 oz Trufree or Jubilee No. 7 S.R. flour (200 g)
2 level tablespoons cocoa *
5 oz caster sugar (130 g)
2 tablespoons treacle
2 eggs
5 tablespoons vegetable oil
5 tablespoons milk

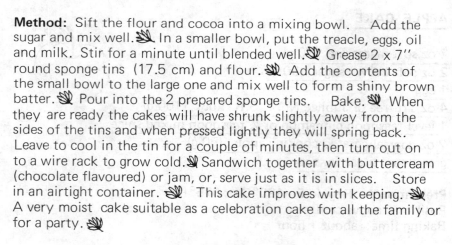

Preheat oven: Regulo 3 (160° C or 300° F)
Position: above centre of oven
Baking time: 45 to 50 minutes

Method: Sift the flour and cocoa into a mixing bowl.   Add the
sugar and mix well.🐝 In a smaller bowl, put the treacle, eggs, oil
and milk. Stir for a minute until blended well.🐝 Grease 2 x 7''
round sponge tins (17.5 cm) and flour. 🐝 Add the contents of
the small bowl to the large one and mix well to form a shiny brown
batter.🐝 Pour into the 2 prepared sponge tins.   Bake.🐝 When
they are ready the cakes will have shrunk slightly away from the
sides of the tins and when pressed lightly they will spring back.
Leave to cool in the tin for a couple of minutes, then turn out on
to a wire rack to grow cold.🐝 Sandwich together with buttercream
(chocolate flavoured) or jam, or, serve just as it is in slices.   Store
in an airtight container. 🐝 This cake improves with keeping. 🐝
A very moist cake suitable as a celebration cake for all the family or
for a party. 🐝

CHOCOLATE BUTTERCREAM   *

2 oz butter (50 g)
4 oz icing sugar, sifted (100 g)
2 heaped teaspoons cocoa*
1 tablespoon milk

Method: Beat the butter with about half the icing sugar. Add the
rest of the icing sugar, the cocoa and the milk. 🐝 Beat until creamy.
Will keep in the fridge for weeks. 🐝

* Must be gluten-free/wheat-free

RICH COFFEE CAKE

Method:

Make and bake as for Rich Chocolate Cake but use 1 tablespoon instant coffee* instead of the cocoa. Make the buttercream with coffee instead of chocolate flavouring (2 level teaspoons instant coffee*). You can also add 6 chopped walnut halves to the filling for variation. 🌿

GINGERBREAD

**

3½ oz Trufree or Jubilee No. 7 S.R. flour (90 g)

1 level teaspoon ground ginger

2½ oz brown sugar (70 g)

1 generous tablespoon black treacle

1 egg

2½ tablespoons vegetable oil

2½ tablespoons milk

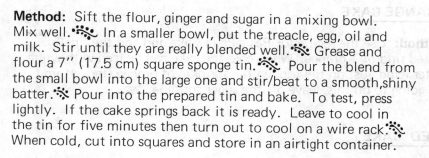

Preheat oven: Regulo 3 (160° C or 325° F)
Position: above centre of oven
Baking time: 45 to 50 minutes

Method: Sift the flour, ginger and sugar in a mixing bowl. Mix well.✷ In a smaller bowl, put the treacle, egg, oil and milk. Stir until they are really blended well.✷ Grease and flour a 7" (17.5 cm) square sponge tin.✷ Pour the blend from the small bowl into the large one and stir/beat to a smooth,shiny batter.✷ Pour into the prepared tin and bake. To test, press lightly. If the cake springs back it is ready. Leave to cool in the tin for five minutes then turn out to cool on a wire rack.✷ When cold, cut into squares and store in an airtight container.

This cake will improve for keeping.✷ A moist cake. If you don't have a square sponge tin, use a round one and cut into wedges instead of squares.

* Must be gluten-free/wheat-free

BASIC PLAIN CAKE — see following recipes for a variety of flavours

All this page ***

2 oz margarine (50 g)

2 oz caster sugar (50 g)

1 egg

4 oz Trufree or Jubilee No. 7 S.R. flour (100 g)

flavouring of choice

Preheat oven: Regulo 5 (190°C or 375°F)
Position: top shelf
Baking time: just under 1 hour

Method: Grease and flour a small loaf tin (traditional 1 lb size).
Put all ingredients into a bowl, including the flavouring you have
chosen and mix/beat with a wooden spoon to a soft, creamy
consistency. If you think it is too stiff then add a little cold milk.
Put the mixture into the prepared loaf tin and bake. After
the first 25 to 30 minutes turn the heat down to Regulo 4 (180°C
or 350°F) for another 20 to 25 minutes to cook the centre.
Let the cake cool in the tin for a minute and then turn out on to
a wire rack to cool. If you wish you can sprinkle the top of the
cake with granulated sugar before you put it in the oven.

Do not overbake this type of cake or it will be too dry. The actual
baking time depends on the type of flavouring used.

ORANGE CAKE

Method: Use the recipe for Basic Plain Cake and add the finely
grated rind of 1 orange. When cold the cake can be iced with white
water icing, just on the top, with a sprinkle of orange rind. If you
are going to do this, leave off the sugar sprinkle.

SEED CAKE

Method: Use the recipe for Basic Plain Cake. Add ½ to 1 teaspoon
caraway seeds, according to taste and 1 teaspoon treacle. Some
people like to eat this type of cake as a teabread, spread with
butter or margarine.

GINGER CAKE

Method: Use the Basic Plain Cake recipe and put in 1 heaped teaspoon dried ginger. 1 teaspoon treacle can also be added. 🍃

CHOCOLATE CAKE

Method: Use the Basic Plain Cake recipe and add 2 heaped teaspoons cocoa* and 1 teaspoon treacle. 🍃

SPICE CAKE

Method: Use the recipe for Basic Plain Cake and add 1 heaped teaspoon mixed spice*. 🍃

COFFEE CAKE

Method: Use the Basic Plain Cake recipe and add 2 slightly heaped teaspoons instant coffee*. Omit the sugar sprinkle. When cold, ice with buttercream icing and decorate with walnut halves. 🍃

CAROB CAKE

Method: Use the Basic Plain Cake recipe and add 2 heaped teaspoons carob powder and 1 teaspoon treacle. Use the shortest cooking time.

MADEIRA CAKE (LEMON CAKE)

Method: Use the Basic Plain Cake recipe and add the finely grated rind of 1 small lemon. 🍃

VANILLA CAKE

Method: Use the Basic Plain Cake recipe and add a few drops of vanilla flavouring. 🍃

*Must be gluten-free/wheat-free

63

MARBLE CAKE

Method: Use the Basic Plain Cake recipe. Take half the mixture and put it into a small bowl. To this add 1 level teaspoon cocoa*. Into the prepared tin drop alternate blobs of the two mixtures until they are all used up. During baking they will amalgamate and produce slices of cake with swirls of brown and yellow.

MARBLE CAKE (3 colours)

Method: Use the recipe for the large version of Basic Plain Cake but do not flavour. Divide the mixture into 3 equal amounts. To the first one add about 3 or 4 drops vanilla flavouring. To the second add 1 level teaspoon cocoa and to the third add 2 drops of red food colouring. Drop blobs of all three flavours into the prepared cake tin. Bake as directed in Basic Plain Cake recipe.

BUTTERCREAM

2 oz butter (50 g)
4 oz sifted icing sugar (100 g)
1 tablespoon milk
flavouring

Method: Beat the butter with about half the icing sugar. Add the rest of the icing sugar, milk and flavouring. Beat until creamy. Will keep in the fridge for several weeks unless fresh fruit is used for the flavouring. Choose from this list:—

Orange — omit milk and add 1 tablespoon fresh orange juice instead.

Lemon — omit half the milk and add 2 teaspoons fresh lemon juice instead.

Coffee — add 1 level teaspoon instant coffee*

Chocolate — see page 60

64

* Must be gluten-free/wheat-free

If you wish to make a larger cake, for all the family, here is a
double size recipe. Make and bake as for Basic Plain Cake
but use a 7" (17.5 cm) round cake tin. For the flavours, here
is a revised list, following the double recipe.

BASIC PLAIN CAKE (LARGE VERSION)   ***

4 oz soft margarine (100 g)

4 oz sugar (100 g)

2 eggs

8 oz Trufree or Jubilee No. 7 S.R. flour

1 tablespoon treacle

flavouring of choice (see following list)

Flavours:

Ginger — 2 heaped teaspoons ground ginger

Chocolate – 1 level tablespoon cocoa*

Orange — finely grated rind of 1 large orange

Seed — 1 heaped teaspoon caraway seeds

Madeira — finely grated rind of 2 small lemons

Coffee — 1 level tablespoon instant coffee*

Carob — 1 level tablespoon carob powder

Vanilla — about 10 drops vanilla flavouring

Spice — 2 heaped teaspoons mixed spice*

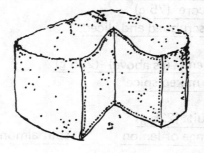

* Must be gluten-free/wheat-free

65

WHOLEFOOD FRUIT CAKES

The following four Fruit Cakes require a special blend of flours
that you can make and store yourself. Blend in a large bowl
and store in a sealed plastic bag, in a cool dry place. Amounts are
given for 1 cake or in bulk, enough for 4 cakes.

Flour blend for 1 fruit cake:

1 oz soya flour (25 g)
4½ oz ground rice, preferably brown (120 g)
½ oz yellow split pea flour (15 g)
2 oz ground almonds (50 g)

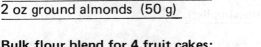

Bulk flour blend for 4 fruit cakes:

4 oz soya flour (100 g)
1 lb 2 oz ground rice, preferably brown (500 g)
2 oz yellow split pea flour (50 g)
8 oz ground almonds (225 g)

WHOLEFOOD DUNDEE CAKE

*****

¼ pint unsweetened orange juice (150 ml)
2 tablespoons brown sugar
¼ oz dried active yeast (7 g)
3 tablespoons sunflower oil
3 oz eating apple, washed and cut into pieces — do not
    peel or remove core (75 g)
1½ oz fresh carrot, scrubbed and sliced

8 oz special flour blend (as above) (225 g)
2 heaped teaspoons mixed spice*

8 oz dried mixed fruit (225 g)
grated rind of 1 orange or lemon   split almonds

66   * Must be gluten-free/wheat-free

Preheat oven: Regulo 4 (180°C or 350°F)
Position: top shelf
Baking time: about 1 hour

Method: Warm the fruit juice and pour into the liquidizer goblet.
Sprinkle in the dried yeast and leave to soften for a few minutes.
❧ Put the oil into a mixing bowl and add the flour blend and the
mixed spice. ❧ Put the apple and carrot pieces into the liquidizer
with the juice/yeast. Blend and pour over the flour mix. ❧ Stir
well and add the fruit and rind. Mix again. ❧ Grease a 7 inch
diameter cake tin (175 mm). Spoon in the mixture and flatten
the top. Decorate neatly with split almonds. ❧ Bake. Leave to
cool in the tin for half an hour. Take out of the tin and finish
cooling on a wire rack. ❧ Keep in an airtight container and
consume within 8 to 10 days. ❧

Although this may seem a strange recipe the end result is very
like a traditional Dundee Cake, rich and moist. Nutritional
value excellent. ❧

WHOLEFOOD RAISIN CAKE

Method: Make as for Dundee Cake but use 8 oz raisins (225 g)
instead of mixed fruit. Omit almond decoration. ❧

WHOLEFOOD CURRANT CAKE

Method: Make as for Dundee Cake but use 8 oz currants (225 g)
instead of the mixed fruit. Best with lemon rind, not orange. ❧

WHOLEFOOD SULTANA CAKE

Method: Make as for Dundee Cake but use 8 oz sultanas (225 g)
instead of the mixed fruit. ❧

WHOLEFOOD APRICOT CAKE

Method: Make as for Dundee Cake but use 8 oz chopped dried
apricots instead of the mixed fruit and 1 heaped teaspoon
cinnamon instead of the mixed spice.

67

CHRISTMAS CAKE — a rich, dark fruit cake — use also for birthday, wedding and christening cake

**

8 oz Trufree or Jubilee No. 7 S.R. flour (225 g)
¼ level teaspoon salt
1 level teaspoon cinnamon
1 heaped teaspoon mixed spice*
2 oz ground almonds (50 g)

4 oz brown sugar (100 g)
6 oz soft margarine (175 g)
2 generous teaspoons black treacle

3 eggs
2 tablespoons sherry
1 lb dried mixed fruit
2 oz raisins   (50 g)
2 oz glacé cherries (50 g)
grated rind of 1 lemon

Preheat oven: Regulo 3 (160°C or 325°F)
Position: middle shelf
Baking time: about 2¼ to 2½ hours

Method: Mix flour, salt, spices and ground almonds. Cream sugar, margarine and treacle. Beat eggs with the sherry and add alternately with the flour to the margarine mixture. Stir in all fruit and lemon rind. Line an 8 or 9 inch diameter cake tin with greased, greaseproof paper (20 to 23 cm). Put the cake mixture into this and flatten with a knife. Bake for 1¼ hours and then lower the heat to Regulo 2 (150° C or 300° F) to cook the centre. Cool in the tin for several hours. Store in a sealed container for about a week before you ice etc. This next bit is optional — for a really moist cake, prick the top with a fork and dribble in more sherry. Spread with   apricot jam after removing paper. Cover with marzipan (see recipe) and ice with royal icing (see recipe). Decorate and serve on a cake board.

68   * Must be gluten-free/wheat-free

MARZIPAN — enough for a 9" cake, top and sides

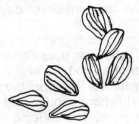

1 lb ground almonds (500 g)
8 oz caster sugar (225 g)
8 oz icing sugar (225 g)
2 teaspoons fresh lemon juice
4 drops almond flavouring
1 large egg, beaten

Method: Mix the ground almonds, caster sugar and icing sugar
in a mixing bowl. ❀ Make a well in the centre and put in the
lemon juice and enough egg to make a firm dough. ❀   Knead into
one ball. Don't overdo it or you will make it too sticky and difficult
to manage. Roll out, using more icing sugar and handling the
marzipan as little as possible. ❀ Use for covering Rich Fruit Cake.

ROYAL ICING — enough for 2 coats and decoration for a 9" cake,
top and sides

3 egg whites
1½ lb icing sugar, sifted (675 g)
1 teaspoon lemon juice
1½ teaspoons glycerine (optional)

Method: Put the egg whites into a bowl and beat with a fork
until frothy. Use a wooden spoon to beat in half the sifted icing
sugar. Now beat until white and smooth while you add the lemon
juice, glycerine and the remaining icing sugar. It should stand in
soft peaks. ❀ Leave for a few hours, covered with a clean cloth
so that any air bubbles can disperse. If you decide to make this
icing with an electric beater you will need to leave for about 24
hours as it will probably have many air bubbles.   Stir with a wooden
spoon before use. ❀

The easiest way to cover a Christmas Cake is to spread cake sparingly
with apricot jam, cover with marzipan and then a thick layer of Royal
Icing. Take a round-ended knife, such as a butter knife and press into

69

the icing. Lift so that a peak forms. Continue all over the cake and leave for a couple of days to harden. ❀

Some people prefer icing on the top of the cake only. This will require half the quantities shown. ❀ Spread top with apricot jam, cover with marzipan and ice with 2 coats of Royal Icing, leaving the first coat to harden for 24 hours before applying the second. When the second coat is hard enough, use the rest of the icing, coloured if you wish, to decorate. Use an icing set with nozzles to give variety and bought decorations. The icing can be kept in the fridge until you need to use it. Always stir before using. ❀ Cover the sides of the cake with a cake frill and stand the cake on a board covered with foil. ❀

ALMOND CAKE

***

2 oz soft margarine (50 g)

2 oz soft brown sugar (50 g)

1 egg

4 oz Trufree or Jubilee No. 7 S.R. flour (100 g)

4 or 5 drops almond flavouring

2 oz ground almond

flaked almonds for the top

Preheat oven: Regulo 5 (190°C or 375°F)
Position: above centre
Baking time: about 1 hour

Method: Grease and flour a small loaf tin (traditional 1 lb size). ✎ Put the first 6 ingredients into a mixing bowl and mix/beat to a soft consistency. Spoon into the prepared tin and sprinkle with flaked almonds. Bake for 30 minutes and then turn the heat down to Regulo 4 (180° C or 350° F) for the last 30 minutes. If the almonds start to look too toasted, cover the cake with greaseproof paper to stop them burning. ✎ Allow to cool in the tin for a few minutes before turning out on a wire rack to cool. ✎ Store in an airtight container. ✎

BASIC FRUIT CAKE MIX

2 oz sugar (50 g)
2 oz soft margarine (50 g)
2 eggs
4 oz Trufree or Jubilee No. 7 S. R. flour (100 g)
rind of ½ lemon, finely grated

4 oz fruit as indicated in following recipes (100 g)

Preheat oven: Regulo 5 (190°C or 375° F)
Position: top shelf
Baking time: 1 hour

Method: Grease and flour a small (traditional 1 lb) loaf tin.
Put all the ingredients into a mixing bowl, except the fruit.
❀ Stir/mix/beat to a soft dropping consistency. ❀ If you
think it is too heavy, add a little milk and beat again.   Stir
in the fruit. ❀ Spoon into the prepared loaf tin and flatten
with a knife. Sprinkle the top with a little sugar if you wish.
Bake for half an hour and then either move the cake down
one shelf or lower the heat to Regulo 4 (180°C or 350° F).
Bake for another half hour. ❀   Leave to cool in the tin
for a minute or two and then turn out on to a wire rack to
finish cooling. When cold store in an airtight container.
Eat within a week of baking.❀

Use the following recipes to vary the fruit and flavour. ❀

MUESLI CAKE

Method: Use the recipe for Basic Fruit Cake. Instead of adding 4 oz
(100 g) of fruit make a mixture of almonds, walnuts, sesame seeds,
sunflower seeds and raisins. If you don't want to guess the amounts
— 1 oz (25 g) each of the nuts and raisins and 1 heaped teaspoon
each of the seeds. Also add 1 generous teaspoon honey to the mix.

RAISIN CAKE

Method: Make and bake as for Basic Fruit Cake Mix. Use raisins for the fruit. ❀

SULTANA CAKE

Method: Make and bake as for Basic Fruit Cake Mix. For fruit use sultanas. ❀

CURRANT CAKE

Method: Use the Basic Fruit Cake Mix. Make and bake using currants for the fruit. ❀

APRICOT CAKE

Method: Make and bake as for Basic Fruit Cake Mix. Use chopped dried apricots for the fruit. Optional — add 1 level teaspoon ground cinnamon. ❀

CHERRY CAKE

Method: Make and bake as for Basic Fruit Cake Mix. Use chopped glacé cherries for the fruit. ❀

MIXED FRUIT CAKE

Method: Use the Basic Fruit Cake Mix, make and bake using 3 oz dried mixed fruit (75 g) and 1 oz glacé cherries, chopped (25 g) and a few drops almond flavouring. ❀

FRUIT SALAD CAKE

Method: Make and bake as for Basic Fruit Cake Mix but use chopped dried fruit salad, taking care to remove prune stones. Also add 1 level teaspoon cinnamon. ❀

DATE AND GINGER CAKE ***

Method: Make and bake as for Basic Fruit Cake Mix but use chopped cooking dates for the fruit and 1 slightly rounded teaspoon dried ginger. ✿

DATE AND WALNUT CAKE ***

Method: Use the recipe for Basic Fruit Cake. Instead of all fruit, use 2 oz chopped cooking dates (50 g) and 2 oz chopped walnuts (50 g). ✿

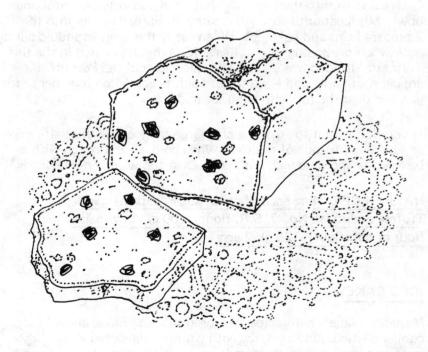

VICTORIA SPONGE (large)

8 oz caster sugar (225 g)

8 oz soft margarine (225 g)

4 eggs

8 oz Trufree or Jubilee No. 7 S.R. flour (225 g)

2 oz maize flour or cornflour* (50 g)

jam

icing sugar

Preheat oven: Regulo 5 (190°C or 375°F)
Position: above centre of oven
Baking time: 20 to 25 minutes

Method: Grease and flour the edges of 2 x 8 inch (20 cm) sponge
tins. Cut out 2 circles of greaseproof paper to fit the bottoms.
Grease and fit into the tins. Put all ingredients into a mixing
bowl. Mix/beat until soft and creamy. * Spread evenly into the
2 prepared tins and bake. When ready the sponges should spring
back when pressed lightly.   Leave for a minute or two in the tins.
Turn out, upsidedown on to a wire rack to cool   Peel off the
greaseproof paper and leave to get cold. * Sandwich together with
jam and dust the top with icing sugar.

If you don't want to make such a large sponge, use this half-recipe
and bake in just one of the tins. When cold. slice through with a
breadknife and sandwich with jam. Dust top with icing sugar.

HALF RECIPE 4 oz each of caster sugar, soft margarine,
Trufree or Jubilee No. 7 S.R. flour (100 g), 1 oz maize
flour or cornflour* (25 g), 2 eggs

ICED CAKE   **

Method: Make a half-recipe flavoured sponge. Bake, allow to
cool and when quite cold, ice with white or flavoured water
icing or a layer of buttercream icing, plain or flavoured.
Decorate with glacé cherries.

* Must be gluten-free/wheat-free

FLAVOURED SPONGES

CHOCOLATE

Method: Make as for Victoria Sponge. For the large recipe add 2 level tablespoons cocoa* and for the small, 1 tablespoon.

GINGER

Method: Make as for Victoria Sponge. For the large recipe add 1 level teaspoon ground ginger and for the small ½ teaspoon.

VANILLA SPONGE

Method: Make the Victoria Sponge recipe. For the large recipe add about 8 drops vanilla flavouring and for the small one about 4 drops.

COFFEE

Method: Make as for Victoria Sponge. For the large recipe add 1 level tablespoon instant coffee* and for the small one, 2 teaspoons.

ORANGE

Method: Make as for Victoria Sponge. For the large recipe add the finely grated rind of 1 orange. For the small recipe add the finely grated rind of 1 small orange.

LEMON

Method: Make as for Victoria Sponge. For the large version add the finely grated rind of 1 lemon. For the smaller recipe add the finely grated rind of ½ a lemon.

* Must be gluten-free/wheat-free

BATTENBURG CAKE

**

Method: Make a half-recipe Victoria Sponge. Divide into two. ✽⤳
Colour one half of the mixture with a few drops pink food
colouring and flavour the other half with 2 or 3 drops vanilla
flavouring. Bake in a square sponge tin with a pleat in the
middle to separate the two flavours. Cool on a wire rack. ✽⤳
When cold, cut neatly into 4 equal sized lengths and sandwich
together so that the colours counterchange , using a spreading
of jam. Roll out the marzipan to fit the cake all round but not
on the ends. Spread with jam, using a pastry brush. ✽⤳ Put the
cake on to the marzipan which is in turn on a sheet of greaseproof.
Use the paper to help you cover the cake. Overlap the join and
make sure this comes at the bottom of the cake. Trim neatly and
serve in flat slices. ✽⤳ Use the marzipan recipe in this section.
Not for beginners, but a spectacular cake if neatly made. ✽⤳

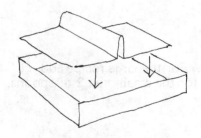

Use greased greaseproof or
silicone paper for the pleated
liner

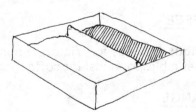

Pleat separates the two colours

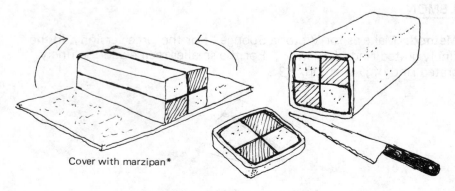

Cover with marzipan*

* Must be gluten-free/wheat-free

THREE TIER SPONGE

Method: Make three flavours of sponge, using the half-recipe
for each one — chocolate, vanilla and plain, coloured pink with
a few drops of food colouring. Bake and allow to cool. Sandwich
together with jam or plain buttercream icing. Ice the top with
white water icing. To make sure you get one completely flat
sponge for the middle layer, spread the uncooked mixture in
the sponge tin so that there is less in the centre and more round
the edges. A simple but very attractive cake. 🍃

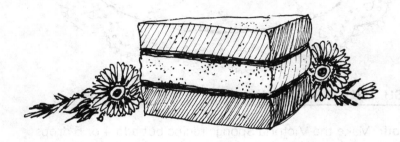

COFFEE GATEAUX

Method: Make the large coffee flavoured Victoria Sponge recipe. 🍃
Sandwich together with coffee buttercream. Spread more
buttercream on the top and decorate with walnut halves
after texturing with a fork. For the Coffee Buttercream you
will need 8 oz sifted icing sugar (225 g), 4 oz butter (100 g),
2 tablespoons milk and 2 heaped teaspoons instant coffee*. 🍃
Make by beating half the icing sugar with the butter until soft.
Add the remaining ingredients and beat to a soft cream. 🍃

* Must be gluten-free/wheat-free

FRESH FRUIT GATEAUX

Method: Make the Victoria Sponge recipe but add 4 or 5 drops vanilla flavouring. When baked and cold, sandwich together with whipped cream and fresh fruit such as sliced strawberries, raspberries, sliced kiwi fruit, fresh (sweet) apricots or peaches, chopped, fresh pineapple etc. Spread more cream on the top and sprinkle the centre with flaked almonds, preferably toasted. Decorate the edge with more of the fruit. Makes a good treat for all the family and an excellent celebration cake.

Small Cakes
and
Buns

BUNS — makes 6 light buns ******

2 oz soft brown sugar (50 g)
2 oz soft margarine   (50 g)
1 egg
2½ oz Trufree or Jubilee No. 7 S.R. flour (70 g)

Preheat oven: Regulo 5 (190°C or 375°F)
Position: top shelf
Baking time: 15 to 18 minutes

Method: Either grease and flour 6 patty tins or line with cake papers. 🍃 Put all ingredients into a bowl and beat to a creamy consistency. Spoon into the patty tins and bake. When ready, remove from oven and leave to cool in the tins for about four or five minutes. Take out of the tins and cool on a wire rack. Store in an airtight container and use within a few days. 🍃

These buns can be flavoured or iced in a variety of ways. 🍃

ORANGE BUNS ******

Method: Add the grated rind of one small orange and make and bake as for Buns. Cold buns can be iced with white water icing or orange icing made with orange juice and icing sugar. 🍃

79

WATER ICING

Method: Sift 4 oz icing sugar (100 g) into a basin and add 1 tablespoon warm water. Mix well. Use to ice a dozen buns or the top of an 8 inch (20 cm) cake or sponge. The icing can be flavoured if desired. Add orange or lemon juice instead of the water for citrus flavours. Sift 1 slightly heaped tablespoon of cocoa* in with the icing sugar for a chocolate flavour. Add 1 teaspoon instant coffee powder* to the warm water for coffee flavour.

LEMON BUNS   All this page **

Method: Make and bake as for Buns but add the finely grated rind of ½ a lemon.

GINGER BUNS

Method: Make and bake as for Buns but add ½ teaspoon dried ginger.

CURRANT BUNS

Method: Make and bake as for Buns but add 1 tablespoon of currants.

APRICOT BUNS

Method: Make and bake as for Buns but add 6 chopped dried apricot halves and ½ level teaspoon cinnamon.

CHOCOLATE BUNS

Method: Make and bake as for Buns but add 1 heaped teaspoon cocoa*. Leave plain or ice with chocolate* for a treat.

FRUIT BUNS

Method: Make and bake as for Buns but add 1 tablespoon dried mixed fruit.

* Must be gluten-free/wheat-free

SPICE BUNS

Method: Make and bake as for Buns but add 1 level teaspoon mixed spice*.

CHERRY BUNS

Method: Make and bake as for Buns but add 6 glacé cherries, chopped.

VANILLA BUNS

Method: Make and bake as for Buns but add a few drops of vanilla flavouring.

COFFEE BUNS

Method: Make and bake as for Buns but add 1 heaped teaspoon instant coffee*. For a treat, ice with white water icing and top with a walnut half.

ALMOND BUNS

Method: Make and bake as for Buns but add 1 heaped teaspoon ground almond and a few drops of almond flavouring. For a treat ice with white water icing and top with an almond.

BUTTERFLY BUNS

Method: Make and bake as for Buns but add a few drops vanilla flavouring. When cold slice off the raised tops and cut in half. Spread the cut part of the bases with a generous portion of buttercream icing and push in the two half pieces as wings. Dust with icing sugar. To make sure you get the right shape buns make into 7 instead of 6 and bake in paper cases.

* Must be gluten-free/wheat-free

RAISIN BUNS   ***

Method: Make and bake as for Buns but add 1 heaped tablespoon
raisins and the finely grated rind of ½ an orange. 🌿

SULTANA BUNS   ***

Method: Make and bake as for Buns but add 1 heaped tablespoon
sultanas and the finely grated rind of ¼ of a lemon. 🌿

CARAWAY BUNS   ***

Method: Make and bake as for Buns but add 1 slightly heaped
teaspoon caraway seeds. 🌿

COCONUT BUNS   **

Method: Make and bake as for Buns but add 1 level tablespoon of
dessicated coconut. If you wish to add more coconut, increase
to 1 heaped tablespoon and make into 7 instead of 6 buns. 🌿

MADELEINES   *

Method: Make and bake as for Buns but add 3 drops vanilla
flavouring. When cold, spread the tops with raspberry or strawberry
jam. Dip into dessicated coconut to cover jam and top with a
half glacé cherry. Easiest to handle if baked in paper cases. 🌿

ROCK CAKES — makes 8 large

***

5 oz Trufree or Jubilee No. 7 S.R. flour (125 g)

2½ oz soft margarine (70 g)

2 ½ oz sugar (70 g)

1 egg, beaten

4 oz dried mixed fruit (100 g)

grated rind of 1 lemon or 1 orange

Preheat oven: Regulo 7 (220°C or 425°F)
Position: top shelf
Baking time 12 to 15 minutes

Method: Rub in the margarine and flour until it resembles breadcrumbs. Stir in the sugar and then the egg. Mix to a sticky paste. ✳ Add the fruit and rind and mix again.✳ Grease and flour a baking sheet and put heaps of the mixture on to it, leaving plenty of space for the buns to spread.✳✳ Sprinkle with granulated sugar and bake until golden. Do not let them brown too much or they will turn out too dry. Cool on a wire rack. Store in an airtight container but eat within a couple of days. ✳

CHERRY CAKES

**

Method: Make and bake as for Rock Cakes but use glacé cherries instead of dried fruit. Chop before using. ✳

NUBBIES

***

Method: Make and bake as for Rock Cakes but for the dried fruit use sultanas OR currants OR raisins and 1 level teaspoon mixed spice.

APRICOT CAKES

***

Method: Make and bake as for Rock Cakes but use chopped dried apricots instead of dried mixed fruit.

FRESH FRUIT CAKES

***

Method: Make and bake as for Rock Cakes but instead of dried fruit use fresh fruit. Remove stones if any and chop flesh. Fruit must be ripe and sweet. Choose from fresh fruit in season — cherries OR apricots OR peaches OR plums OR blackberries (especially brambles) OR pineapple. ❀

DATE CAKES

Method: Make and bake as for Rock Cakes but instead of dried fruit use chopped cooking dates. If these are not available then use eating dates with the stones removed. ❀

BASIC SWEET DOUGH — for Bath Buns, Currant Buns etc.

***

10 oz Trufree or Jubilee No. 4 white flour (275 g)
¼ oz instant yeast
2 oz sugar (50 g)
3 pinches salt
fruit and flavouring of choice (see recipes that follow)
2 oz margarine
5 fluid oz warm water

Preheat oven: Regulo 7 (220°C or 425°F)
Position: above centre of oven
Baking time: 15 to 20 minutes

Method: Put the flour, yeast, sugar and salt into a bowl. Put in the spice (if any) and mix well. ❀ Rub in the margarine. Add the appropriate fruit and the warm water. ❀ Mix with a wooden spoon to a sticky paste. ❀ Wet the hands and divide the dough into equal portions according to the recipe you have chosen. ❀ Roll into balls, without using more flour, flatten slightly and place on a greased baking sheet. ❀ Leave to rise in a warm place. ❀ When doubled in size bake until golden brown.   Cool on a wire rack.   Serve warm or freshly baked, or, split and toasted with butter. ❀❀❀

84

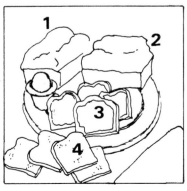

BREAD

1. Trufree Brown Bread made with No. 5 flour
2. Trufree White Bread made with No. 4 flour
3. Bread and Butter
4. Toast

SPONGE CAKES — made with Trufree
or Jubilee No. 7 S.R. flour

1. Victoria Sponge
2. Iced Buns

SHAPED, CRUSTY BREAD ROLLS
easily made with Trufree or Jubilee
No. 4 flour

1. Sesame Rolls
2. Small Cottage Loaf
3. Knot
4. Finger Rolls

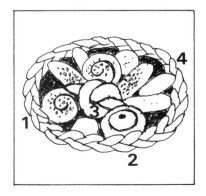

FRUIT BREADS

1. Currant Bread using Trufree No. 4 flour
2. Currant Bread using Trufree No.5 flour

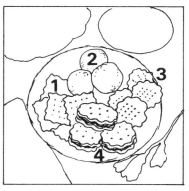

BISCUITS

1. Cheese wafers
2. Ginger Nuts
3. Rich Shortbread
4. Bourbon Creams

BREAD AND SCONES

1. Trufree Bread from the baker
2. Plain Scones
3. Fruit Scones
4. Cheese Scones
5. Soda Bread

BAKING with Trufree and Jubilee Flours — Wheat-free/Gluten-free

Top left to right: Trufree Bread, Victoria Sponge, Soda Bread, Plait, French Stick. Middle left to right: Shaped Bread Rolls, Hot Cross Buns, Sponge Buns, Iced Buns, Danish|Pastries, Crumpets, Cheese Scones, Viennese Fancies, Breadsticks. Bottom left to right: Langues de Chat, Currant Buns, Fruit Scones

PARTY FOOD

1. Savoury Choux Buns
2. Home-made Soup
3. Canapés
4. Savoury Tartlets
5. Cocktail Biscuits

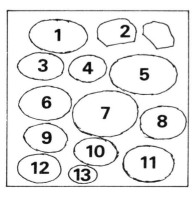

GLUTEN-FREE AND WHEAT-FREE
BAKING with Trufree/Jubilee Flours

Used here for:— 1. White and Brown Bread. 2. White and Brown Currant Bread. 3. Buttered Currant Bread. 4. Cherry Cake and Fruit Pie. 5. Savoury Tartlets, Choux Buns, Sesame Crackers, Crispbread and Plain Crackers. 6. Rich Shortbread, Bourbon Biscuits (Creams), Cheese Wafers and Ginger Nuts. 7. Iced, Plain and Chocolate Buns. 8. Brown and White Bread and Butter. 9. Fruit Crumble. 10. Profiteroles. 11. Lemon Pancakes. 12. Canapés. 13. Cocktail Biscuits.

YEASTED BUNS

1. Currant Buns
2. Danish Pastry
3. Chelsea Buns
4. Hot Cross Buns

SHAPED BREADS — made with Trufree or Jubilee No. 4 flour

1. French Stick
2. Plait
3. Sesame Rolls
4. Breadsticks

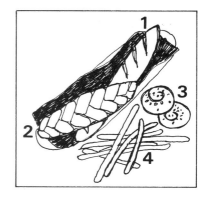

RICH FRUIT CAKE

Used here for Christmas Cake (made with Trufree or Jubilee No. 7 S.R. flour) this recipe also makes a suitable base for Wedding, Christening, Anniversary and Birthday Cakes. It can be handed round confidently as it is impossible to distinguish from similar cake made with wheat flour. Cover with marzipan and ice with Royal Icing for a real Celebration Cake.

SAVOURY BISCUITS

1. Crackers
2. Sesame Crackers
3. Crispbreads

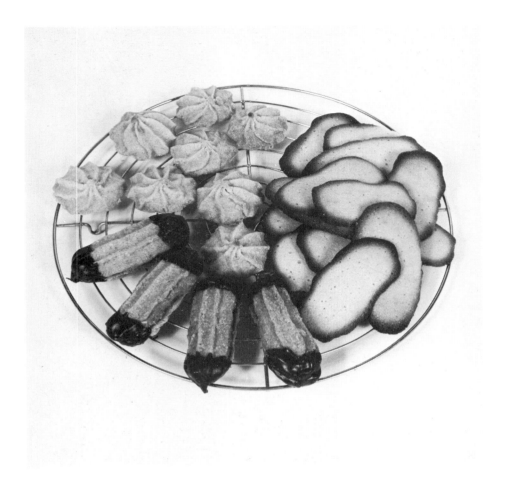

BISCUITS

1. Viennese Fancies — 2 shapes
2. Langues de Chat

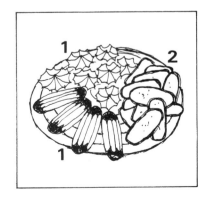

CRUMPETS

Use Trufree or Jubilee No. 4 flour for these. They are easy to
make and really delicious. Can be made in advance and toasted
just before they are eaten.

PUDDINGS

1. Profiteroles
2. Fruit Crumble
3. Fruit Pie
4. Fresh Fruit Tartlets
5. Lemon Pancakes

GLAZE FOR BUNS

Method: Put 2 tablespoons milk into a small saucepan with 2 tablespoons caster sugar (or soft brown sugar). Bring to the boil for a few seconds and then simmer for 2 minutes. Brush over hot buns with a pastry brush. Leave to set for a few minutes. 〜

HOT CROSS BUNS   ****

Method: Make the Basic Sweet Dough. For spice add 1 level teaspoon each of cinnamon and mixed spice*. For fruit use 2 oz currants (50 g) and 1 oz mixed peel (25 g). ❀ Make into 10 buns. Make a shallow cross on each one with a sharp knife. (When the buns are baked the cross will be pale cream and the tops of the buns brown.) Leave to rise in a warm place, on a greased baking tray. Bake. Glaze as soon as you take them out of the oven. ❀A traditional item eaten on Good Friday and during Easter.❀Serve warm, freshly baked. ❀

FRUIT BUNS   ****

Method: Make the Basic Sweet Dough. Use dried mixed fruit — 2 to 3 oz (50 to 75 g). The grated rind of 1 small lemon or orange can also be added (optional). ❧ Serve warm or cold, freshly baked. ❧ Split and butter. Delicious toasted and buttered. ❧ Glaze as soon as they are baked. ❧ Makes a dozen buns. ❧

BATH BUNS   ***

Method: Use the Basic Sweet Dough recipe. To flavour use the finely grated rind of 1 small lemon. For the fruit use 2 oz sultanas and 1 oz chopped mixed peel (50 g and 25 g).❀Before you put the buns into the oven, brush with beaten egg and sprinkle with crushed lump sugar, the traditional topping.❀Makes 8 large buns.❀ Some people will prefer slightly less sugar in the dough — 1½ oz instead of 2 oz (40 g instead of 50 g). ❀ ❀❀

* Must be gluten-free/wheat-free

85

TEACAKES

Method: Make as for Fruit Buns but make into 6 large buns (fairly flat). Serve split, toasted and buttered while still warm. Glaze as soon as they are out of the oven. ✂➤

CURRANT BUNS

Method: Make the Basic Sweet Dough. Use 3 oz of currants (75 g) and (optional) the grated rind of a small lemon. Serve warm from the oven, split and buttered. Can also be served toasted. Glaze as soon as they are baked. ❀ Makes a dozen buns. ✂

BASIC DOUGH — for Chelsea Buns and Danish Pastries

10 oz Trufree or Jubilee flour No. 4 (white) (275 g)
¼ oz instant yeast (7 g)
4 fluid oz warm water (120 ml)
2 pinches salt
4 drops almond flavouring
2 oz margarine (50 g)
2 oz sugar (50 g)
1 oz ground almonds (25 g)

Preheat oven: Regulo 5 (190° C or 375° F)
Position: above centre of oven
Baking time: 20 minutes

Method: Put the flour, yeast, salt and almond flavouring into a bowl with the sugar and ground almonds. Mix.❀ Add the margarine and rub in with the fingers. ❀ Pour in the water and mix to a sticky dough. ❀ Take out of the bowl and knead on a cool worktop without using more flour. When the dough is smooth and shiny it is ready to use — this will take about 3 or 4 minutes. Do not use flour for shaping. ❀   Continue as directed in the following recipes. ❀

86

CHELSEA BUNS   ***

Method: Make up the Basic Dough recipe, adding ½ teaspoon mixed spice*, the finely grated rind of ½ a lemon and 2 oz currants (50 g) to the flour. 🌸 Divide into 12 equal portions after kneading. Roll out each one into a long sausage.   Sprinkle with a little brown sugar and roll up into a coil.🌸 Leave to rise on a greased baking tray, in a warm place, making sure the buns have room to spread a little.🌸   When doubled in size, bake. As soon as you take them out of the oven, glaze. (See Glaze for Buns recipe). Eat warm or cold, but always freshly baked.🌸

DANISH PASTRIES (filled)   ***

Method: Make up the Basic Dough recipe, adding 3 or 4 pinches ground cardamom to the flour.🌸 Divide into 8 equal pieces and roll out into long sausages on a cool worktop. Spread with one of the suggested fillings and roll up into coils.🌸 Lay on a greased baking sheet and leave to rise in a warm place. Bake and glaze as for Chelsea Buns. Eat freshly baked. 🌸 (The cardamom is optional).

Fillings:
1. Mix equal quantities of butter, brown sugar and ground almonds to a cream.
2. Grate eating apple and mix with sugar
3. Mincemeat (see recipe in this book) mixed with ground almonds.

DANISH PASTRIES (topped)   **

Method: Make up the Basic Dough, adding 2 oz dried mixed fruit to the flour.🌸 Divide into 10 pieces equal in size and roll out into long sausages. Roll up into wheels or double coils and place on a baking sheet, in a warm place, to double in size. Bake when ready. For a transparent top spread with icing made with icing sugar and hot water, as soon as they come out of the oven. For a white top, leave to get almost cold. Ice with white water icing, sprinkle with flaked almonds and pieces of glacé cherry. Eat freshly baked. 🌸

* Must be gluten-free/wheat-free

ECLAIRS

Method: Make and bake as for Choux Pastry (see section on pastry and puddings) but make into 6 finger shapes on the baking sheet. When cold, fill with whipped cream and top with chocolate water icing. Eat soon after they are made. 🌼

CREAM PUFFS

Method: Make and bake as for Choux Pastry (see section on pastry and puddings) but make into 4 heaped mounds on the baking sheet. Leave plenty of room for them to spread. 🌼 When cold, fill with whipped cream to which you have added 3 or 4 drops vanilla flavouring and ½ level teaspoon icing sugar. Dust the tops with icing sugar. Eat soon after they are made. 🌼

ECCLES CAKES — makes 4 or 5

Shortcrust Pastry — see recipe in Puddings and Pastries Section
½ oz margarine (15 g)
2 heaped teaspoons brown sugar
2 oz currants (50 g)
1 oz dried mixed peel (25 g)
¼ level teaspoon mixed spice*

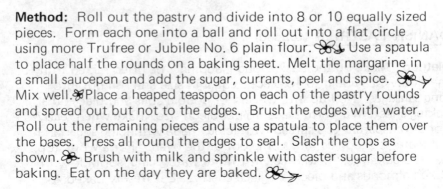

Preheat oven: Regulo 7 (220°C or 425°F)
Position: above centre of oven
Baking time: about 15 minutes

Method: Roll out the pastry and divide into 8 or 10 equally sized pieces. Form each one into a ball and roll out into a flat circle using more Trufree or Jubilee No. 6 plain flour. 🌼 Use a spatula to place half the rounds on a baking sheet. Melt the margarine in a small saucepan and add the sugar, currants, peel and spice. 🌼 Mix well. 🌼 Place a heaped teaspoon on each of the pastry rounds and spread out but not to the edges. Brush the edges with water. Roll out the remaining pieces and use a spatula to place them over the bases. Press all round the edges to seal. Slash the tops as shown. 🌼 Brush with milk and sprinkle with caster sugar before baking. Eat on the day they are baked. 🌼

*Must be gluten-free/wheat-free

RING DOUGHNUTS — makes about 10

6 oz Trufree or Jubilee No. 4 white flour (175 g)
1 level teaspoon cream of tartar
1 level teaspoon bicarbonate of soda
3 pinches salt
1 oz soft margarine
1 oz caster sugar (25 g)
3 fluid oz water (90 ml)

Method: Mix the flour, cream of tartar, bicarbonate of soda and salt, in a bowl. Add the margarine and rub in. Stir in the sugar and water. Mix to a sticky dough. Make a ball of dough the size of a walnut. Flatten by hand on a floured surface to this thickness [   ] and shape a hole in the centre. Use a spatula to lift it and slide it into hot, deep fat or oil. The ring will sink to the bottom and, as the dough expands, rise to the top. Turn with kitchen tongs so that it fries evenly on both sides. Drain on kitchen paper and sprinkle with caster sugar. Best eaten warm.

NB. If the fat is too hot the doughnuts will brown on the outside and will not be cooked on the inside. You will find once you have heated the oil sufficiently it can be turned down to a much lower heat just to keep the temperature steady. If the doughnut rises to the surface immediately then this is a sign that the oil is too hot.

JAM DOUGHNUTS – makes 12 to 15 small doughnuts **

8 oz Trufree or Jubilee No. 4 flour (225 g)
¼ oz instant yeast (7 g)
4 fluid oz warm milk or water (120 ml)
2 heaped teaspoons caster sugar
3 pinches salt
1 oz margarine
1 egg, beaten
red jam
more caster sugar for sprinkling

Method: Put the flour, yeast and salt into a basin. ✿ Add the margarine and rub in with the fingers. Combine the egg and warm milk or water. Mix into the flour. ✿ Leave to rise in a warm place for about 15 minutes. ✿ Take the dough out of the bowl and knead on a floured* surface. Divide into 12 to 15 equal sized pieces. Either roll into balls and flatten slightly or shape in 'sausages'. Leave to rise on a greased baking sheet, in a warm place. ✿ When doubled in size, loosen carefully with a knife and drop into hot oil. ✿ Deep fry for about a minute on each side. ✿ Drain and cool on a wire rack. ✿ Serve split, filled with jam and dusted with caster sugar. Alternatively, split, fill with jam and fresh whipped cream and dust with icing sugar. Use the sausage-shaped ones for the latter. Eat freshly baked. ✿

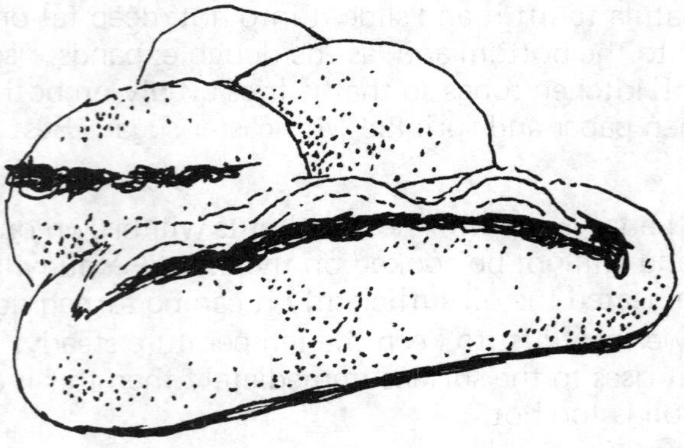

Puddings
and
Pastries

FRUIT

The easiest and perhaps the best kind of puddings are just fresh fruit. An eating apple, a small banana and half an orange, sprinkled with a little brown sugar and moistened with orange juice can be enjoyed all the year round. In summer it can be varied with soft fruits such as strawberries and raspberries, kiwi fruit, apricots, plums and peaches. 🐝

Other fruits can be stewed in a little water with honey or brown sugar to taste. Apple is always a favourite and combines well with other fruits such as blackberries, plums and apricots. Red and blackcurrants, gooseberries and damsons can be bought at reasonable prices as they near the end of their short seasons. 🐝

If you have fallen into the trap of thinking that you must put some kind of gooey concoction smothered in cream on the table everyday as a pudding, please think again. Save yourself lots of hassle in the kitchen and just put a bowl of fresh fruit on the table instead. 🐝

SUMMER PUDDING — serves 1 ***

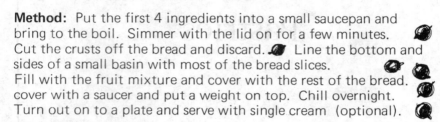

2 oz raspberries (50 g)
2 oz red or blackcurrants, prepared (50 g)
1 tablespoon water
1 level tablespoon sugar
3 thin slices special bread* (white) made with
    Jubilee or Trufree No. 1 or No. 4 flour

Method: Put the first 4 ingredients into a small saucepan and bring to the boil. Simmer with the lid on for a few minutes. Cut the crusts off the bread and discard. Line the bottom and sides of a small basin with most of the bread slices.
Fill with the fruit mixture and cover with the rest of the bread. cover with a saucer and put a weight on top. Chill overnight. Turn out on to a plate and serve with single cream (optional).

It is important to have the correct size basin. The pudding should fit into it so that it reaches the top. The weight and saucer will stop the pudding expanding as the bread soaks up the fruit juice and makes sure the pudding is firm.

FRUIT ON BREAD ***

1 portion of stewed and sweetened plums, greengages,
    apricots or damsons
2 slices special bread*
oil for frying

Method: Fry the bread in hot oil, on both sides. Put on to a hot plate and top with the stewed fruit which should also be hot. Serve immediately. A very simple but delicious sweet. Serve to the family using ordinary bread and to the special dieter using special bread. Cook the fried bread for the special dieter first and keep hot under a low grill until ready to top with the fruit. For a special treat serve with a little single cream.

* Must be gluten-free/wheat-free

APPLE CHARLOTTE

***

6 thin slices bread* made with Jubilee or Trufree flour
    No 4 or 5
melted butter or margarine
sugar (brown)
1 large cooking apple, peeled and cored
squeeze of lemon juice (fresh)

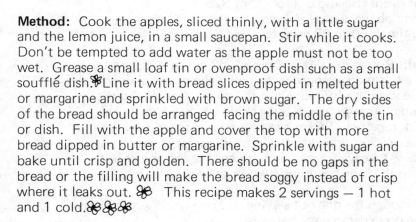

Preheat oven: Regulo 5 (190°C or 375°F)
Position: top shelf
Baking time: about 30 minutes

Method: Cook the apples, sliced thinly, with a little sugar
and the lemon juice, in a small saucepan. Stir while it cooks.
Don't be tempted to add water as the apple must not be too
wet. Grease a small loaf tin or ovenproof dish such as a small
soufflé dish. Line it with bread slices dipped in melted butter
or margarine and sprinkled with brown sugar. The dry sides
of the bread should be arranged facing the middle of the tin
or dish. Fill with the apple and cover the top with more
bread dipped in butter or margarine. Sprinkle with sugar and
bake until crisp and golden. There should be no gaps in the
bread or the filling will make the bread soggy instead of crisp
where it leaks out.   This recipe makes 2 servings — 1 hot
and 1 cold.

FRUMBLE

***

1 slice bread* made with Jubilee or Trufree flour Nos 1,4 or 5
½ oz butter or margarine (15 g)
1 portion hot stewed and sweetened fruit
sugar

Method: Crumble the bread by hand to coarse crumbs. Melt
the butter or margarine in a frying pan and sprinkle in the
crumbs. Fry while turning them over with a spatula. When
crisp and golden put on top of the hot fruit. Sprinkle with
sugar and serve.   A quick and easy special pudding — enough
for 1 person.

* Must be gluten-free/wheat-free

BREAD AND BUTTER PUDDING

6 slices white bread made with Jubilee or Trufree flour
   (No. 1 or No. 4 flour)

1 oz butter (25 g)

1 oz sultanas or currants (25 g)

1 oz caster sugar (25 g)

1 egg

½ pint milk (300 ml)

grated nutmeg

Preheat oven: Regulo 3 (160°C or 325°F)
Position: above centre of oven
Baking time: 50 to 60 minutes

Method: Butter the slices of bread and cut in half. Arrange
half in a buttered ovenproof dish with the butter side down.
Sprinkle with the fruit and half the sugar. Cover with the
remaining buttered bread, butter side up. ❀❯ Beat the egg
and milk together. Strain over the pudding through a fine
mesh sieve. Sprinkle with the remaining sugar and nutmeg
to taste. ❀❯ Leave for half an hour for the egg and milk to
soak into the bread and swell. ❀❯ Bake until golden. ❀❯

Makes enough for one hot serving and one cold. A good way
of using up expensive special bread.

FRITTERS

2 oz Trufree or Jubilee No. 7 S.R. flour (50 g)

1 egg

one eighth of a pint of milk (75 ml)

pinch salt

teaspoon of oil

sliced cooking apple, peeled and cored or bananas sliced
   lengthways and then in half

oil for frying

sugar for sprinkling

Method: Put the flour and egg into a basin and mix/beat to a stiff paste. Gradually add the milk , salt and oil (1 teaspoon) while you beat. Continue beating until you have a smooth, thick batter. Dip the prepared fruit into the batter so that it is completely covered. Fry in hot oil and serve right away, crisp and golden, sprinkled with sugar. 🕸

STEAMED SPONGE PUDDING — basic recipe ✱✱

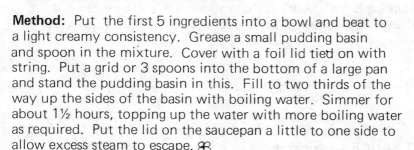

| 4 oz caster sugar   (100 g) |
| 4 oz margarine (100 g) |
| 2 eggs |
| 4 oz Trufree or Jubilee No. 7 S.R. flour   (100 g) |
| 1 oz maize flour or cornflour* (25 g) |
| flavouring, fruit or topping of choice |

Method: Put the first 5 ingredients into a bowl and beat to a light creamy consistency. Grease a small pudding basin and spoon in the mixture. Cover with a foil lid tied on with string. Put a grid or 3 spoons into the bottom of a large pan and stand the pudding basin in this. Fill to two thirds of the way up the sides of the basin with boiling water. Simmer for about 1½ hours, topping up the water with more boiling water as required. Put the lid on the saucepan a little to one side to allow excess steam to escape. 🕸

When ready to serve take off the foil and cover with a hot plate. Turn up-side-down and take off the basin. Serve with custard or suitable sauce. 🕸 The following variations will all be popular!

Fruit Toppings: Before you put the sponge mixture into the basin, spoon in prepared stewing fruit such as apple, plum, raspberries, greengages, blackberries, damsons, black or red-currants or any mixture. 🕸 Sprinkle with sugar to taste. 🕸

Jam or Treacle Toppings: Before you put the sponge mixture into the basin, spoon in 3 tablespoons of jam or treacle. Serve with more jam or treacle, heated in a saucepan. 🕸

* Must be gluten-free/wheat-free

Dried Fruit Fillings: Fold in any of the following dried fruits. You will need about 4 oz (100 g). Sultanas, raisins, currants, mixed fruit, stoned prunes, chopped apricots, chopped dates or chopped fruit salad. ❀❀ ❀

Flavours:

Ginger — Add ½ level teaspoon dried ginger to the sponge mixture. Serve with custard. ❀ ❀ ❀

Chocolate:— Add 2 heaped teaspoons cocoa* to the sponge mixture. Serve with Chocolate Sauce*. Combine this flavour sponge with a fruit topping of pears or apple, for variation. ❀❀❀

Orange — Add the finely grated rind of 1 orange to the sponge mixture. Serve with Orange Sauce or custard.* ❀❀ ❀

Lemon — Add the finely grated rind of 1 lemon to the sponge mixture. Serve with Lemon Sauce* or Vanilla Sauce.* ❀ ❀❀

A rib-sticking British pudding that will serve 4, can be eaten hot or cold and is good enough to serve to the whole family. ❀❀❀

SWEET SAUCE — basic recipe

1 oz maize flour or cornflour* (25 g)
1 pint milk (575 ml)
1 slightly heaped tablespoon sugar

Method: Take a little of the milk and put into a small jug with the flour. Put the rest of the milk into a saucepan with the sugar and bring to the boil. Remove from heat and pour in the milk/flour mix. Stir well and return to heat. Simmer while stirring for another 3 to 4 minutes. Add the flavouring of your choice and stir in well. Serve hot, in a jug, poured over hot puddings. ❀

* Must be gluten-free/wheat-free

CHOCOLATE SAUCE **

Make the Sweet Sauce and add 2 heaped teaspoons cocoa* as the flavouring. Some people prefer more cocoa than this.

VANILLA SAUCE **

Make the Sweet Sauce and add about 6 or 7 drops vanilla flavouring or drops to taste.

ORANGE OR LEMON SAUCE **

Make the Sweet Sauce and add either the juice and rind of half a lemon or the juice and rind of a whole orange.

JAM SAUCE *

Heat any flavour of jam in a small saucepan with a little water. Stir well and serve hot.

FRUIT SAUCE ***

Heat sweetened stewed fruit that has been puréed in a blender. If too thick, thin down with a little water. Serve hot. If too thin sprinkle in a teaspoon or two of ground rice. Heat and stir to thicken. Serve hot.

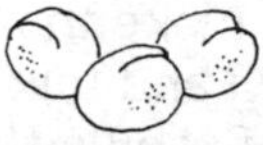

BAKED ALASKA – serves 4 *

Method: Make a base from a Victoria Sponge (½ recipe) using the recipe from the cakes section. Cut it through and sandwich together generously with jam. Cut it into an oblong or square or just make it into a smaller round. Put on to an ovenproof pie plate. Make the meringue as for Lemon Meringue Pie with 2 egg whites and 4 oz caster sugar (100 g). Pile home-made vanilla ice cream on top of the base and cover with the meringue, using a palette knife. The meringue must cover the sponge and ice cream completely. If there is a hole anywhere the ice cream will melt and run out. Bake immediately in a very hot oven at Regulo 8 (230°C or 450°F) for a mere 3 to 4 minutes. Serve right away. An amazing sweet but not for beginners.

* Must be gluten-free/wheat-free

PINEAPPLE UPSIDEDOWN PUDDING — serves 4 generously **

Topping:

soft margarine

2 oz brown sugar (50 g)

4 slices tinned pineapple (rings) well drained

4 glacé cherries

Base:

4 oz each of caster sugar, soft margarine and Trufree or
   Jubilee No. 7 S.R. flour (100 g of each)

1 oz maize flour or cornflour*

2 eggs

Preheat oven: Regulo 5 (190°C or 375°F)

Position: above centre of oven

Baking time: 20 to 25 minutes

Method: With margarine, liberally grease a straight-sided, shallow round dish about the size of a sponge tin. (A Pyrex flan dish is ideal). Sprinkle all over with the brown sugar and arrange the pineapple rings in it, as shown. Put a cherry into the centre of each pineapple ring. Now make the base. Put all ingredients for the base into a mixing bowl and mix/beat to a soft consistency. If preferred add a few drops of vanilla flavouring — 4 or 5. Carefully spoon the base over the topping making sure you fill all the gaps between the pineapple rings. Flatten with a knife. Bake. Leave to cool in the dish. When required, put a plate on top of the dish. Hold the two firmly together and turn upside-down. Shake the pudding on to the plate. To make it extra special, decorate with rosettes of piped cream.

Far less trouble than making a gateaux and just as impressive. Eat on the day of baking. Serve to the whole family.

Variation:

Use fresh pear halves instead of the pineapple rings. Make the base and add 2 heaped teaspoons cocoa* and a little milk if it turns out too stiff.

* Must be gluten-free/wheat-free

98

EVE'S PUDDING — 3 to 4 servings
***

Topping:
2 oz soft margarine (50 g)
2 oz sugar (50 g)
2 oz Jubilee or Trufree No. 7 S.R. flour (50 g)
½ oz maize flour or cornflour* (15 g)
1 egg

Base:
8 oz peeled, sliced cooking apples (225 g)
sugar to taste

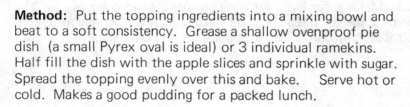

Preheat oven: Regulo 5 (190° C or 375° F)
Position: top shelf
Baking time: 20 to 25 minutes

Method: Put the topping ingredients into a mixing bowl and beat to a soft consistency. Grease a shallow ovenproof pie dish (a small Pyrex oval is ideal) or 3 individual ramekins. Half fill the dish with the apple slices and sprinkle with sugar. Spread the topping evenly over this and bake. Serve hot or cold. Makes a good pudding for a packed lunch.

The fruit base can be varied and any one of the following or any mixture of them is suitable — plum, blackcurrant, blackberry and apple, greengage, damson, gooseberries, red or white currants, apricots, raspberries and peaches. You will need 8 oz fruit (225 g). Dried Fruit can also be used if soaked overnight and drained before use. Try dried fruit salad, prunes or apricots.

Variations:

PEAR AND CHOCOLATE PUDDING
***

Method: Make as for Eve's Pudding but use cooking pears for the base. For the topping substitute cocoa* for the maize or cornflour.

* Must be gluten-free/wheat-free

99

RHUBARB AND GINGER PUDDING   ***

Method: Make as for Eve's Pudding but use rhubarb instead of apple for the base. For the topping add ½ level teaspoon ground ginger.

SPICED APRICOT PUDDING   ***

Method: Make as for Eve's Pudding but used halved, stoned apricots instead of apple for the base. For the topping add ¼ teaspoon cinnamon.

CHERRY AND VANILLA PUDDING   ***

Method: Make as for Eve's Pudding but use stoned cherries instead of apple for the base. Add 4 to 5 drops vanilla flavouring to the topping mixture. Serve sprinkled with caster sugar.

BAKED BANANAS   *****

For each person:—
1 banana, halved lengthways
sprinkle of soft brown sugar
1 tablespoon fresh orange juice
knob of butter or margarine

Preheat oven: Regulo 4 (180°C or 350°F)
Position: near top of oven
Baking time: about 15 minutes

Method: Arrange banana slices in a greased ovenproof dish. Spoon over the juice and sprinkle with sugar to taste. Bake and serve hot from the oven. The bananas may discolour a little but this does not affect the taste. A delicious yet simple pudding.

SHERRY TRIFLE — serves 4 or 5

4 plain sponge buns* or 2 slices Victoria Sponge*
jam
3 egg yolks
2 slightly heaped teaspoons maize flour or cornflour*
1 oz caster sugar (25 g)
¾ pint milk
4 tablespoons sherry
2 bananas
¼ pint double cream, whipped (150 ml)
glacé cherries and toasted almond flakes for decoration

Method: Slice the sponge cakes or sponge and spread with
jam. Arrange at the bottom of a serving dish, preferably a
glass one. Beat the egg yolks, cornflour and sugar until smooth.
Bring the milk just to the boil in a saucepan and pour on to the
egg yolk mixture. ❀ Stir well. ❀ Return to the saucepan and
heat gently while you stir. Continue until the custard is thick
enough to coat the back of a wooden spoon. Cool a little. ❀
Use a spoon to dribble the sherry over the sponge cake. Slice
the bananas and lay on the top. ❀ Pour the custard over them
and leave to set. ❀ When quite cold and set, spread a layer of cream
over the top. Pipe cream rosettes around the edge and decorate
with the cherries cut into quarters and the almond flakes. ❀

Variations: Decorate with Ratafias. These are made with the
Almond Macaroon recipe and are very small versions of the full-
size macaroons. ❀ The fruit can also be varied according to
season. Fresh peaches, peeled and stoned then cut into small
slices are very good. ❀

A very rich dessert suitable for celebrations but not everyday use.
If making for children omit the sherry and call it 'Fruit Trifle'. ❀

* Must be gluten-free/wheat-free

STEAMED PUDDING

Pastry:

2 oz soft margarine (50 g)

4 oz ground rice (100 g)

3 oz grated eating apple (75 g)

Filling:

8 oz raw stewing fruit (225 g)

sugar to taste

1 tablespoon water

Method: Put the pastry ingredients into a bowl and blend with a fork. Make into a stiff paste by kneading with the fingers, using more ground rice if the paste is too sticky. ✿ Grease a 1 pint (575 ml) pudding basin generously with margarine. Take two thirds of the pastry and roll into a ball. Flatten and place at the bottom of the basin. With the fingers, press the pastry round and up the sides of the basin so that it is lined as evenly as possible to just ½ inch below the rim (12 mm). Make the remaining one third of the pastry into a round, flat lid by pressing flat with the fingers.
✿ Cut the fruit into thin slices and put layers of these, sprinkled with sugar, into the lined basin. Fill almost to the top of the pastry, spoon over 1 tablespoon water and lift on the lid with a spatula. Press the edges on to the lining to seal it. ✿ Tie on a foil lid with suitable string and make a string handle too. ✿ Have ready a large saucepan of boiling water, one third full. Put a grid or 3 spoons (metal) into the bottom to keep the basin off the bottom of the pan. Lower the basin into the water and put the lid on the pan. ✿ ✿ Steam for only ¾ of an hour, topping up the water level with more boiling water, as required. ✿ When ready, take out of the pan and remove string and foil. Put a warm plate over the top of the pudding and holding the two firmly together, turn upside down. Don't shake it but leave for a few seconds. The pudding will drop on to the plate. Take off the basin carefully and serve pudding hot with custard.* ✿

For fruit filling — gooseberries, blackberry and apple, apple on its own, pears, apricots or any mixture. Plums are also suitable.✿ This pudding tastes just like a suet/wheat flour pudding yet it has the advantage of not being high in fat and taking far less time to steam. Good for cold winter days and very popular with children.

* Must be gluten-free/wheat-free

CRUNCHY DATE TART

****

Pastry:

2 oz soft margarine (50 g)

4 oz ground rice (100 g)

3 oz finely grated eating apple (75 g)

Filling:

4 oz chopped cooking dates (100 g)

teacup full of water (approx)

1½ oz chopped walnuts (40 g)

sprinkle of sunflower seeds

Preheat oven: Regulo 7 (220° C or 425° F)
Position: top shelf
Baking time: 20 to 25 minutes

Method: Put the dates into a small saucepan with the water and cook until they form a stiff paste. Leave to cool. Use a fork to blend the pastry ingredients then knead in the bowl until the dough forms one ball. Grease a pie plate and put the dough in the centre. Flatten with the palm and fingers until it has spread evenly over the bottom. Raise a slight edge all the way round by pressing with the fingers. With a knife, spread the date mixture over the pastry, inside the raised edge. Sprinkle with the nuts and sunflower seeds, pressing them slightly into the dates. Bake. Eat hot or cold when the pastry will be crisper. Although there is no sugar in this recipe it is very sweet, rather like treacle tart.

Can also be made with dried apricots (soaked overnight), a sprinkle of cinnamon and flaked almonds.

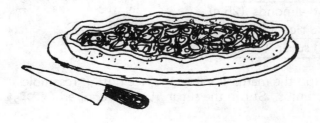

CRUMBLE TOPPINGS (for fruit)

These toppings are easy to make and can be stored in an airtight container, in the fridge, until required. Just sprinkle a generous layer over stewed, sweetened fruit and bake for 10 to 12 minutes in a preheated oven Regulo 8 (230° C or 450° F), until golden brown. Before baking, make a hole through to the fruit to allow the steam to escape and stop the fruit spilling over the edges and spoiling the top. Bake on the top shelf and use small ovenproof dishes. Serve hot or cold.

Any kind of fruit in season is suitable — apples, rhubarb, apricots, plums, gooseberries, blackcurrants, blackberry and apple, stewing pears, raspberries or any mixture. Dried Fruit Salad can also be used, dried apricots and prunes.

PLAIN CRUMBLE   ***

3 oz margarine (75 g)
6 oz ground rice (150 g)
2 oz sugar (50 g)

Method: Rub the margarine into the rice. Stir in the sugar.

NUT CRUMBLE   ****

1 tablespoon cooking oil
1 oz ground almonds (25 g)
4 oz ground rice (100 g)
1 oz brown sugar (25 g)

Method: Rub the margarine into the rice until it resembles fine breadcrumbs. Stir in the sugar. Use as required.

104

LUXURY CRUMBLE

3 oz margarine (75 g)

6 oz ground rice (150 g)

2 oz sugar (50 g)

1 heaped tablespoon sunflower seeds

1 heaped tablespoon sesame seeds

1 heaped tablespoon chopped walnuts

1 oz ground almonds (25 g)

Method: Rub in the margarine and rice until it resembles breadcrumbs. Stir in all the other ingredients.

REAL FRUIT JELLY

¾ pint fruit juice or any liquidized stewed fruit juice, diluted
    with water (425 ml)

½ oz unflavoured gelatine (15 g)

sugar to taste

Method: Put about 3 tablespoons of the fruit juice into a small saucepan. Sprinkle in the gelatine. Stir well making sure you get rid of all the lumps. Heat very gently and gradually bring to the boil while you stir. Pour into the rest of the juice and mix well. Now add sugar to taste, making sure it dissolves too. Pour into 4 individual glasses or one dish to set. Serve cold from the fridge.

Fresh fruit can be liquidized with a little water and strained to remove pips — raspberries and strawberries are excellent. Try blends of two or three juices for variety such as orange, pineapple and strawberry. Fruits with a strong flavour are best. Dried fruits can be soaked, stewed and liquidized. Try stoned prunes with a little lemon juice or dried apricots with orange juice.

FRUIT SALAD PIE

***

Pastry:

2 oz soft margarine (50 g)

4 oz ground rice (100 g)

3 oz finely grated eating apple (75 g)

1 heaped teaspoon brown sugar

3 good pinches cinnamon

Filling:

8 oz dried fruit salad (225 g)

water

1 heaped teaspoon ground rice

¼ level teaspoon cinnamon

1 heaped teaspoon brown sugar

squeeze fresh lemon juice

Preheat oven: Regulo 8 (230°C or 450°F)
Position: top shelf
Baking time: about 25 minutes

Method: Wash the fruit salad. Drain and cut out the prune
stones. Cut all the fruit into smaller pieces and put into a medium
saucepan with enough water to cover, the heaped teaspoon ground
rice and the cinnamon. Bring to the boil and add the sugar and
lemon juice. Cook steadily with the lid on for 15 minutes. ✿⌣
✿⌣ Blend the pastry ingredients with a fork and knead into
1 ball of dough. Grease a small oval pie dish with margarine. ✿⌣
✿Take two thirds of the pastry and line the inside of the dish,
pressing the pastry out by hand to a little above the rim of the
dish.✿⌣ Flatten out the remaining pastry into an oval shape,
about the size of the pie. Cut into quarters with a knife. ✿⌣
✿⌣ Sprinkle the bottom of the pastry case with ground rice.
Spoon in the hot fruit without too much liquid.✿ With a
spatula place the 4 pastry sections so that the outer edges are
touching the edge of the pastry lining. They should leave a
cross shape, as shown, without any pastry covering to let out
the steam during baking. ✿ Pinch the outer edges together neatly.
Bake for 10 minutes and then turn down the heat to Regulo 6
(200°C or 400°F) for another 15 minutes. The pastry should be

crisp and golden. Sprinkle with caster sugar and serve hot, straight from the oven. Warm up any juice that was left in the saucepan and serve with the pie.

Variations: Instead of fruit salad use partly cooked Bramley apples with 3 or 4 pinches ground cloves instead of the cinnamon. Omit the cinnamon from the pastry.

BAKED APPLE

***

1 large cooking apple
stuffing from the list below
soft brown sugar
2 tablespoons water

Preheat oven: Regulo 4 (180°C or 350°F)
Position: above centre of oven
Baking time: about 50 minutes

Method: Wash the apple and remove the core with an apple corer, from top and bottom so you have a hole right through. With a sharp knife make a shallow cut around the middle to let out the steam. This can be cut in a zig-zag line if you prefer. Mix the stuffing you have chosen and fill the hole, pressing it in tightly. Now put the apple in an ovenproof dish and add the water. Bake until soft and serve hot. (If you are baking bread on the same oven setting put in this pudding as well).

Stuffings:—

1. Few sultanas mixed with a little ground almond and a sprinkle of mixed spice and brown sugar.
2. Few chopped dried apricots, pinch or two of cinnamon or ground cloves, sprinkle of sugar and sesame seeds.
3. 1 tablespoon mincemeat* (see recipe on page 140).
4. Sprinkle finely chopped walnuts, few raisins, a little grated lemon rind, brown sugar.

If just cooking a plain baked apple, sprinkle with brown sugar before putting in the oven. There is no need to stuff the centre.

* Must be gluten-free/wheat-free

FRUIT MERINGUE — for 1

**

1 portion stewed, sweetened fruit such as blackberry and
    apple, apple, plum, apricot, greengage etc.
1 egg white
4 level teaspoons caster sugar

Preheat oven: Regulo 3 (160°C or 325°F)
Position: top shelf
Baking time: about 20 minutes

Method: Put the fruit into a small ovenproof dish. Whisk the egg white until stiff and then whisk in the sugar. Pile on top of the fruit and bake. ❁ Serve hot or cold. ❁

FRUIT BRÛLÉE

**

1 portion stewed fruit, sweetened to taste
½ carton natural yoghurt
3 teaspoons soft brown sugar

Method: Put the stewed fruit into an individual-sized ovenproof dish. Pour or spoon the yoghurt over the fruit. Sprinkle the sugar evenly over the top of the yoghurt. Chill in the fridge until required. Place under a hot grill until the sugar melts, watching it carefully as it must not burn. Serve right away. This recipe is for 1 serving.

FRUIT FOOL

**

4 oz stewing fruit (100 g) such as blackcurrants,
    redcurrants, raspberries, apricots, greengages,
    plums, gooseberries, blackberries, rhubarb etc.
2 to 3 tablespoons water
sugar to taste
1 small carton natural yoghurt

Method: Prepare the fruit — wash, top and tail, stone, peel as necessary. Put into a small saucepan with the water (except for rhubarb which will not need any) and sugar to taste. 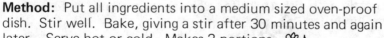 Heat and simmer with the lid on, until tender. Allow to cool. Put into a blender with the yoghurt and blend. Serve in a glass dish with either boudoir fingers* or langues de chat*.

CHOCOLATE RICE PUDDING ***

1 oz pudding rice (short-grain) (25 g)
2 level teaspoons cocoa*
2 heaped teaspoons brown sugar
14 fluid oz milk (400 ml)

Preheat oven: Regulo 2 (150°C or 300°F)
Baking time: 2½ to 3 hours
Position: above centre of oven

Method: Put all ingredients into a medium sized oven-proof dish. Stir well. Bake, giving a stir after 30 minutes and again later. Serve hot or cold. Makes 2 portions.

FRUIT YOGHURT ***

1 small carton natural yoghurt
2 heaped tablespoons prepared , fresh fruit
sugar or liquid honey to taste

Method: Chop the fruit if too large. Fold into the yoghurt and sweeten to taste. Serve chilled from the fridge. Suitable fruits are: orange, satsuma, grapefruit, kiwi fruit, strawberries, raspberries, stoned cherries, stoned apricots or peaches, black-berries, eating apple, pear, melon. Cooked stoned prunes and cooked dried apricots can also be used.

You will find this quite different from commercially made fruit yoghurt which can sometimes contain gluten/wheat in the thickening. It should be less sweet than the fruit fool and the fruit should be in small pieces, not in a purée. Ideal for packed meals and picnics, as a pudding or snack.

* Must be gluten-free and wheat-free

RICH SHORTCRUST PASTRY — makes 6 tartlets or 8 pastry cases

**

4 oz Trufree or Jubilee No. 6 Plain flour (100 g)

1½ oz soft margarine (40 g)

1 egg yolk

2 tablespoons water (cold)

Preheat oven: Regulo 7 (220°C or 425°F)

Position: above centre of oven

Baking time: about 12 to 15 minutes

Method: Put the flour into a basin. Rub in the margarine. Add the egg yolk and water and mix to a sticky paste. Knead into 1 ball using more of the flour. Roll out on a floured surface. Cut into rounds and use a spatula to transfer to 8 patty tins. Bake blind or fill as recipes direct. Eat freshly baked.

To line a dish, put the whole amount of dough into the middle and press out with the fingers until the dish is evenly lined. Trim off edge neatly with a sharp knife. Bake as for tartlets but for an extra 2 or 3 minutes.

TART DU JOUR   **

Method: Make the Rich Shortcrust Pastry dough. Roll out on a baking sheet. Cut to a neat shape and with the fingers, raise a slight rim all round the edge.   Prick with a fork and bake. Allow to cool on the baking sheet and then put carefully on to a serving dish. Make a glaze with apricot jam, a little fresh lemon juice and water to thin down the jam. Heat in a small saucepan and apply with a brush. Cover the base of the cooked pastry and arrange fresh fruit such as strawberry halves, seedless grapes, slices of kiwi fruit, raspberries, slices of ripe apricots or peaches or any selection in season. Arrange in rows and glaze. Allow to set for a few minutes and serve right away. You may find that the glaze needs straining before use. Be as liberal as you can with it, especially on the fruit. A simple but delicious sweet or treat.

110

MINCE PIES

***

Method: Make the Rich Shortcrust dough and roll out. Cut into
6 rounds and line patty tins. Re-roll remaining pastry and cut into
6 small rounds for lids. Spoon in a filling of Sweet Mincemeat*(see
recipe in Extras Section). Place the lids on top. Brush with water
and sprinkle with caster sugar before baking as for Rich Shortcrust
Pastry.

LEMON MERINGUE PIE   **

pastry dough (see Rich Shortcrust Pastry recipe)
2 oz maize flour or cornflour* (50 g)
½ pint water (300 ml)
1 oz butter or margarine (25 g)
grated rind and juice of 2 lemons
2 eggs, separated
6 oz caster sugar (175 g)

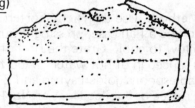

Preheat oven: Regulo 6 (200°C or 400°F)
Position: above centre of oven
Baking time: 15 minutes for pastry case + 25 minutes for meringue

Method: Line an 8 inch flan dish (20 cm) with the pastry, pressing
out thinly with the fingers. Trim with a knife and bake blind.
Remove from oven and turn down the heat to Regulo 3 (160° C
or 325°F). Put the maize flour into a small saucepan and blend with
a little of the water. Pour in the rest of the water and add the margarine or butter. Stir while you bring to the boil and cook for 3
minutes. Remove from heat. Put in the lemon juice and rind.
Add the egg yolks and just 2 oz of the sugar (50 g). Stir these
in well and pour into the flan case.   Next whisk the egg whites
until very stiff. Whisk in half the remaining sugar. Fold in the last
of the sugar with a metal spoon. Spread over the filling making sure
it is covered completely, or it will leak over the meringue and spoil
the pie. Sprinkle the top with a little caster sugar for a crisp finish.
Bake on the lower heat and serve warm or cold. Bake for the whole
family.

* Must be gluten-free/wheat-free

FRUIT FLAN

pastry dough (see Rich Shortcrust Pastry recipe)

1 lb prepared fruit — ripe plums, apricots or peaches (450 g)

brown sugar

Method: Line a flan dish by pressing out the dough with the fingers. 🍂Trim with a knife. 🍂 Cut the fruit into slices and arrange in the flan case. Sprinkle with sugar to taste and bake at Regulo 7 (220°C or 425°F) for 20 minutes, above centre of oven. Serve hot or cold. 🍂

TREACLE TART   *

Method: Use the Rich Shortcrust Pastry recipe to make the dough to line a flan case, pressing it out with the fingers. After baking allow to cool. Grate the rind of 1 lemon into a bowl and place over a saucepan of hot water.   Add the juice of the lemon, 5 generous tablespoons golden syrup and 2 slices of fresh bread made from Trufree or Jubilee No 1 or No 4 flour, made into breadcrumbs.🌼 Stir well and spoon into the pastry case. Bake on the middle shelf of the oven for about 20 minutes at Regulo 5 (190°C or 375°F). Serve hot or cold. 🌼

CHOCOLATE MOUSSE   *

3 oz plain cooking chocolate* (75 g)

3 eggs, separated

2 tablespoons sherry

3 tablespoons whipped cream (optional)

Method: Put a bowl over a pan of hot water. Break the chocolate into pieces and put into the bowl to melt. When melted and stirred, add the egg yolks with the sherry. Mix well. 🐚 Whisk the egg whites until they are quite stiff.   Carefully fold them into the chocolate mixture. Divide into 4 little dishes and leave to set in the fridge. Decorate with the cream if you wish. 🐚

A very rich sweet, for grownups only. Easy to make but impressive!

*Must be gluten-free/wheat-free

112

SHORTCRUST PASTRY

	Half Recipe
8 oz Trufree or Jubilee No. 6 Plain flour (225 g)	4 oz (100 g)
2 pinches salt	1 pinch
3 oz soft margarine (75 g)	1½ oz (40 g)
5 tablespoons cold water	2½ tbs

Preheat oven: Regulo 7 (220°C or 425°F)
Position: top shelf
Baking time: about 20 minutes

Method: Mix the flour with the salt in a mixing bowl. Rub in the margarine until the mixture resembles breadcrumbs. Add the water and mix to a sticky paste. (The water releases the binder from the flour.) Knead gradually, adding only a very small amount of extra flour, until one ball of dough has formed and the bowl is clean. ❀

This pastry is easiest to use for small items which can be cut out of rolled out dough and lifted off the worktop with a spatula. Use to line patty tins. ❀

For larger items such as pies and pasties the dough should be rolled out between sheets of greaseproof paper or silicone paper. The top paper is then peeled off and the pastry turned upsidedown over the dish allowing the backing sheet to peel off. Excess should be trimmed off with a knife and any breaks can be pressed together. The pastry lid should then be rolled out in the same way and dropped on to the filled pie. ❀

If preferred, the bottom part of pies can be pressed out with the fingers as for Rich Shortcrust Pastry and the top rolled out between sheets of greaseproof or silicone paper. Alternatively the top can be made of cut out shapes, using rolled out pastry. ❀

JAM TARTS

Method: Make either Rich Shortcrust Pastry or Shortcrust Pastry dough. Roll out and cut into rounds. Place in patty tins and put a teaspoonfull of jam into each one. Bake as directed for the pastry you have chosen. Serve hot or cold. A good way of using up spare pastry so as not to waste it.

CUSTARD TART

a pastry case, baked blind, made with Shortcrust Pastry in an
   8 inch (20 cm) flan dish (see recipe in this section)

½ pint milk (300 ml)

1 egg yolk

1 egg

1 level tablespoon caster sugar

grated nutmeg

Preheat oven: Regulo 4 (180°C or 350°F)
Position: centre of oven
Baking time: about 20 minutes for large tart and 10 minutes for
   small ones

Method: Heat the milk but do not let it boil. Beat the egg and
sugar in a basin. Pour in the hot milk and stir well. Carefully
pour into the baked pastry case and bake after sprinkling the
top with grated nutmeg. Serve warm or cold but eat on the day
it is baked. Can also be made in small pastry cases (tarts).

FRUIT PIE

***

Method: Make up the half-recipe for Shortcrust Pastry*. Use about
two thirds of the dough to line a small oval pie-dish by pressing
out the dough with the fingers. Roll out the lid between two sheets
of greaseproof paper. Fill the lined dish with prepared and sliced
fruit — blackberry and apple, pear, plum, greengage, apricot, damson
etc, or any mixture in season. If the fruit is ripe put it straight in
the dish. If is it unripe then stew it in a little water for a few minutes
to soften it. Strain and put into the dish. Sprinkle with sugar to
taste. Brush the edges of the pastry with water. Peel off the
top sheet of greaseproof paper. Turn the pastry upsidedown on to
the filled pie. Peel off the paper. Trim with a knife and press the
edges together. Cut a slit in the top, brush with milk and sprinkle
with granulated sugar. Bake for about 20 minutes as for
Shortcrust Pastry. Serve hot or cold.

114   *See page 113

BAKEWELL TART

pastry dough — use either Shortcrust or Rich Shortcrust Pastry
2 tablespoons raspberry jam
2 eggs separated
3 oz fresh breadcrumbs (75 g) made from Trufree or Jubilee
    No. 1 or No. 4 flour bread
3 oz caster sugar (75 g)
4 tablespoons melted margarine
4 oz ground almonds (100 g)
grated rind and juice of 1 lemon
pinch salt

Preheat oven: Regulo 7 (220°C or 425°F)
Position: centre of oven
Baking time: about 30 minutes

Method: Line an 8 inch flan ring or shallow dish (20 cm) with the pastry, pressing it out by hand. Trim with a knife. ✿ Spread the jam over the base. ✿ Put the egg yolks into a basin and beat well. ✿ Add the breadcrumbs, sugar, melted margarine, lemon rind and juice. ✿ Mix well. ✿ Put the egg whites into a bowl with the pinch of salt and beat until stiff. Fold into the other mixture. Spread evenly over the jam and bake until golden and firm. ✿ Serve hot or cold. ✿

FRUIT TARTLETS

**

Method: Make the Shortcrust Pastry dough. ➤ Cut into an equal number of large and small rounds, after rolling out. Use a spatula to line patty tins. Fill with prepared fruit (fresh) or small pieces of stewed fruit. ➤ Sprinkle with sugar and put on the lids. ➤ Bake for about 10 minutes in a preheated oven at Regulo 7 (220°C or 425°F), top shelf. Serve hot or cold. ➤ Makes 12 tartlets or 6 if you use the Half Recipe. ➤

PLATE APPLE PIE
***

Method: Make the Shortcrust Pastry dough. Divide into 2 equal pieces. Roll out one piece between two sheets of greaseproof paper. Remove the top sheet. Turn an ovenproof pie plate upsidedown over the pastry. Hold the two together and turn the right way up. Peel off the paper and trim the edge of the pastry with a knife. Leaving an uncovered ring around the edge, cover the centre with thinly sliced cooking apple, a sprinkle of sultanas, a sprinkle of cinnamon and sugar to taste. Roll out the rest of the pastry between the greaseproof paper. Peel off the top layer. Brush the edge of the pastry on the plate with water. Turn the pastry on the greaseproof upsidedown and place it over the pie. Let it drop on to the fruit and pastry. Seal the edges and make a hole in the centre to let out the steam during baking. Brush with water and sprinkle with caster sugar. Bake as for Shortcrust Pastry. Serve hot or cold.

This can also be filled with prepared blackcurrants or sweet mince-meat (see recipe in Extras Section).

EASY APPLE PIE
***

Method: Make up the Shortcrust Pastry recipe. Line a medium-sized pie dish (a shallow one) with half of the pastry by pressing the dough out with the fingers. Press it up the sides too and trim off excess with a knife. Peel and core a couple of large cooking apples. Slice thinly into the prepared dish and sprinkle with sugar. Also add 3 pinches of powdered cloves if preferred. Roll out the remaining pastry into one piece and cut into small rounds with a cutter. Place around the edge of the pie, overlapping as shown. Brush with water and sprinkle with caster sugar before baking at Regulo 7 (220° C or 425° F), above centre of oven for about 25 minutes. Serve hot or cold.

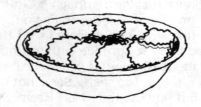

CHEESECAKE — 6 servings **

4 to 6 biscuits* depending on size — digestives* or gingernuts*
1 oz butter (25 g)
1 orange
1 tablespoon fresh lemon juice
½ oz gelatine crystals (1 sachet) (14 g)
12 oz cottage cheese (350 g)
1 small carton natural flavour yoghurt
1½ oz caster sugar (40 g)
2 egg whites
fruit for decoration

Method: Grease an 8 inch (20 cm) flan ring and put it on a
flat plate. Make the biscuits into crumbs — either by grinding
for a few seconds in an electric coffee grinder or by crushing
with a rolling pin between two sheets of greaseproof paper. ✿
✿ Melt the butter in a small saucepan. Stir in the biscuit
crumbs and then sprinkle over the plate, inside the flan ring,
to form the base. Grate an orange and put the grated rind
into the blender. Squeeze out the juice and pour into a small
pan with the lemon juice. Sprinkle in the gelatine. ✿ Heat
very gently until the crystals have dissolved. Add to the orange
rind in the blender and put in the cheese, yoghurt and sugar. ✿
✿Blend until smooth. Whisk the egg whites until stiff. Fold
them into the cheese mixture until it is smooth again. Carefully
spoon the cheese mixture over the crumb base, levelling the top
with a knife. Put into the fridge to set. When ready to serve
decorate the top with orange slices, strawberries, raspberries or
Kiwi fruit as available. Serve to the whole family as a sweet or
at a party. ✿

This recipe is low in fat, making it far less rich and much easier
to digest than the usual kind of cheesecake. A good way of using
up stale special biscuits. ✿

* Must be gluten-free/wheat-free

TRADITIONAL CHRISTMAS PUDDING

***

4 oz Trufree or Jubilee No. 6 plain flour (100 g)

2 oz breadcrumbs made from any Trufree or Jubilee Bread (50 g)

1 teaspoon mixed spice*

1 level teaspoon cinnamon

1 level teaspoon ground nutmeg

4 oz hard margarine (100 g)

4 oz brown sugar (100 g)

4 oz grated apple (100 g)

1 small grated carrot

4 oz mixed peel (100 g)

2 eggs

4 oz currants (100 g)

8 oz raisins (225 g)

2 oz dried apricots (50 g)

4 oz chopped shelled almonds (100 g)

grated rind of 1 small lemon and juice of same

grated rind of 1 orange

1 generous tablespoon black treacle

¼ pint sherry (150 ml)

2 teaspoons thin soy sauce* to darken pudding (optional)

Method: Put all ingredients into a bowl (melt the margarine).
Stir well and leave overnight. Put into two small or one large
pudding basin and cover with foil tied on with suitable string.
Steam for 6 to 8 hours, keeping the water level topped up.
(See Steamed Pudding for use of grid etc). Allow to get
cold and remove foil lid(s). Put on new, dry covers and store
in a cool, dry place. Steam for another 1½ to 2 hours on
Christmas Day. It is impossible to tell the difference between
this recipe and a wheat flour/wheat bread one, so make for the
whole family and friends. However, it will be at its best just
a week after making. Serve hot with Brandy Butter. Some
people like it with custard as well.

* Must be gluten-free/wheat-free

BRANDY BUTTER

4 oz unsalted butter (100 g)
6 oz icing sugar (175 g)
4 tablespoons brandy

Method: Cream the butter until white. Gradually add the sugar and brandy, beating all the time. Put in the fridge to harden up. Serve on hot Christmas Pudding.

CHOUX PASTRY for éclairs, buns, profiteroles etc.   ***
— makes 12 éclairs

4 oz Trufree or Jubilee No. 7 S.R. flour (100 g)
¼ pint water (150 ml)
½ teaspoon sugar
1 oz margarine (25 g)
4 teaspoons cooking oil
2 eggs, beaten

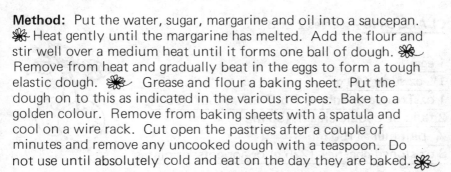

Preheat oven: Regulo 6 (200°C or 400°F)
Position: middle shelf
Baking time: about 20 minutes

Method: Put the water, sugar, margarine and oil into a saucepan. Heat gently until the margarine has melted. Add the flour and stir well over a medium heat until it forms one ball of dough. Remove from heat and gradually beat in the eggs to form a tough elastic dough. Grease and flour a baking sheet. Put the dough on to this as indicated in the various recipes. Bake to a golden colour. Remove from baking sheets with a spatula and cool on a wire rack. Cut open the pastries after a couple of minutes and remove any uncooked dough with a teaspoon. Do not use until absolutely cold and eat on the day they are baked.

If using for savoury recipes such as Savoury Choux Buns, leave out the sugar. The same applies to Yorkshire Puddings using this type of pastry.

PROFITEROLES

Method: Make the Choux Pastry recipe. Put small dollops on to the prepared baking sheets. You should have enough pastry for about 2 dozen. Bake for about 15 minutes. When cold fill with whipped double cream and dribble the special chocolate sauce over them (see next recipe). ✿

CHOCOLATE SAUCE FOR PROFITEROLES   *

6 oz cooking chocolate* (175 g)
¼ pint water (150 ml)
1 teaspoon instant coffee powder*
4 oz sugar (100 g)

Method: Break the chocolate into pieces and put into a small pan with the coffee and 2 tablespoons of the water. ✿ Heat very gently until the chocolate has melted. Add the rest of the water and the sugar. Heat gently while you stir until dissolved. ✿ Now simmer for about 10 minutes. Leave to cool. ✿ This will give you the fairly runny sauce you need for Profiteroles. ✿

CLAFOUTIS — serves 2 or 3   **

1 egg
1½ oz sugar (40 g)
1 oz Trufree or Jubilee No. 7 S.R. Flour (25 g)
2 fluid oz double cream (50 ml)
¼ pint milk (150 ml)
8 oz stoned cherries (225 g) or apricots, or plums

Preheat oven: Regulo 5 (190°C or 375°F)
Position: above centre of oven
Baking time: about 35 minutes

120   * Must be gluten-free/wheat-free

Method: Use a whisk to cream the egg and sugar in a basin. Add the flour in one go. Beat it in and then add the cream and milk. Put the prepared fruit into a shallow ovenproof dish. Pour the batter over the fruit and bake. Serve hot or cold. 🍂

This is a cross between a custard and a cake. It can also be cooked in a pastry case if preferred although this makes it a much heavier type of pudding. Some people like it served with cream but it is best on its own. 🍂

PEACH MELBA — serves 1   **

1 medium-sized ripe, sweet peach
1 heaped tablespoon raspberries
1 heaped tablespoon redcurrants
water
sugar to taste
1 level teaspoon maize flour or cornflour*
1 small portion ice-cream*, homemade, vanilla flavour
2 langues de chat* or boudoir fingers*

Method: Put the raspberries and redcurrants into a small pan with 2 or 3 teaspoons sugar and a tablespoon water. Heat while you stir. Cook until mushy and put through a fine mesh sieve. ❀ Put the resulting juice back into the pan. Mix the maize or cornflour in a cup with a tablespoon water. Add to juice in the pan. Heat and stir until thickened — about 3 minutes. Allow to cool. ❀❀ Peel the peach, stone and cut into quarters. Put a spoonful of the red sauce into a glass dish, cover with the peach quarters and top with more sauce. Top with ice-cream, decorate with the biscuits and serve. Some people will prefer cream over the top as well but this sweet is delicious without it. Not to be compared with the commercially made Peach Melba made with tinned peaches, chemical sauce and bought ice cream! ❀

* Must be gluten-free/wheat-free

BUDGET ICE CREAM

1 small tin condensed milk
½ pint evaporated milk (275 ml)
¼ pint ice-cold water (150 ml)
3 drops vanilla flavouring (150 ml)

Method: Chill the can of condensed milk in the fridge for an hour. Whip the evaporated milk until thick. Mix the condensed milk into the cold water. Fold into the whipped evaporated milk with the flavouring. Freeze until thick , using a metal container. Turn out into a cold bowl and beat until smooth. Put back into the container and freeze again. Repeat and store in the freezer until required. The freezer setting for normal storage is suitable for this ice cream.

Use for a sweet with langues de chat biscuits* and for peach melba. Serve a small portion with fresh fruit salad.

CHOCOLATE PUDDING — 2 servings, hot or cold

***

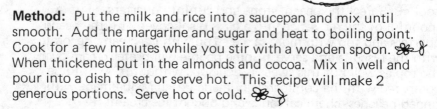

½ pint milk (275 ml)
2 slightly heaped tablespoons ground rice
knob of soft margarine
1 slightly heaped tablespoon sugar
1 level tablespoon ground almonds
1 level tablespoon cocoa*

Method: Put the milk and rice into a saucepan and mix until smooth. Add the margarine and sugar and heat to boiling point. Cook for a few minutes while you stir with a wooden spoon. When thickened put in the almonds and cocoa. Mix in well and pour into a dish to set or serve hot. This recipe will make 2 generous portions. Serve hot or cold.

* Must be gluten-free/wheat-free

Party Foods
and
Packed Meals

Food appropriate for parties appears in several sections of this book. Look for Celebration Cakes, Gateaux, Cocktail Biscuits, Cheese Nibbles, Crispbreads and Water Biscuits. Tart du Jour, Clafoutis, Hamburgers, Choux Buns, Eclairs etc.

Use the recipes in this book for all the special items. i.e. Don't bother to prepare 2 kinds of food, ordinary and special. Make one lot for everyone and save a lot of extra work and worry. You will find the parties planned to include a good deal of ordinary food. Don't underestimate the pleasure a special dieter will get from going to a party where everything on the menu is safe to eat and where everybody else can eat and enjoy his or her type of food. The nicest thing anyone can say is "I wouldn't mind being on your diet if the food is as nice as this."

Packed Meals are included in the section because parties are really only picnics enjoyed at home and packed meals are picnics eaten away from home. With the exception of savoury tartlets and items made with choux pastry all the party foods recipes are suitable for packed meals. Soup can be put into a thermos if required. Bases for canapés can be packed separately from spreads and assembled just before they are eaten. Quiches can be made in individual sizes and wrapped in foil to be eaten cold. Salads should be packed dry with dressing in a separate container to be used just before eating.

CANAPÉS
***

Bread Base: Trufree flours Nos 4 and 5 probably   make the
best bread for these (white and brown). Cut medium thick slices,
remove crusts and cut into triangles or fingers. Fry in shallow,
hot oil, such as sunflower oil, until golden. Fry on both sides
and drain on kitchen paper. When cold, spread with any of the
following pâtés and spreads. ⤳ These fried bread bases do not
go soggy like toast but remain crisp for several hours. As well as
pâtés and spreads, small sardines can be drained of oil, spread with
mayonnaise* and garnished with small slices of tomato or egg
topped with a sprinkle of cress or parsley. ⤳

Biscuit Base: Use the Water Biscuit or the Crispbread recipe from
this book. Roll out the dough and cut into smallish round shapes,
or, large fluted round shapes cut into 4 with a knife. Bake and
when cold, spread with butter or margarine and then one of the
spreads or pâtés that follow. Decorate with sliced hardboiled
egg, tomato, watercress, cress, small onion rings or parsley. The
butter/margarine will act as a barrier to stop the biscuits going
soggy. ⤳

MUSHROOM PÂTÉ
***

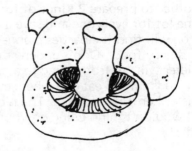

1 small onion, peeled and sliced
1 heaped teaspoon butter
4 oz mushrooms (100 g)
1 small clove garlic, peeled
2 teaspoons thin soy sauce*
1 tablespoon single cream
salt and freshly ground black pepper
1 teaspoon finely chopped fresh parsley

Method: Fry the onion gently in the butter until transparent. ⤳
Wash and slice the mushrooms and add to the pan, turning them
over as you cook them for 3 minutes. Crush in the garlic and
spoon in the soy sauce. Allow to cool for about 5 minutes and
then blend to a creamy paste with the cream. If it turns out too
thin to spread, return to pan and heat gently while stirring to
reduce it. Season to taste and add the chopped parsley. Serve
spread thickly on bread or biscuit bases*. Garnish with parsley or

124

* Must be gluten-free/wheat-free

a sprig of watercress. Don't be put off by the dreary colour — it is really delicious. Also good in sandwiches, especially with brown bread*. ◌

LIVER PÂTÉ   ***

½ lb chicken livers (225 g)
1 small onion or shallot, chopped very finely
1 oz butter
3 good pinches dried mixed herbs
1 small clove garlic, peeled
salt and freshly ground black pepper
teaspoon sherry or white wine

Method: Wash the livers, cutting out stringy parts and yellow pieces. Dry thoroughly and chop into small pieces. Sprinkle with salt and pepper. 🍃 Fry the onion in the butter, using a small saucepan, but don't let it brown. Put in the chopped livers, herbs and garlic — crushed through a garlic press. Turn up the heat a little and stir with a wooden spoon. The livers will start to crumble and start to turn a pinky-brown colour. Add the sherry or white wine. The actual cooking of the livers will take only about 5 minutes. Take off the heat and continue mashing with a fork until you have a smooth paste. When cold, put into small dishes and cover. Store in the fridge and eat within a couple of days. 🍃 Use to make canapés, serve hot with special toast* and butter or spread in sandwiches. Garnish with egg slices and parsley. 🍃

NUT PÂTÉ   ***

4 oz ground almonds (100 g)
2 tablespoons sunflower oil,or similar
2 teaspoons tomato purée, slightly heaped
good squeeze fresh lemon juice to taste
salt and freshly ground black pepper

* Must be gluten-free/wheat-free

Method: Put the ground almonds and oil into a small bowl and blend with a fork. Add the tomato purée and lemon juice. Season to taste, adding more lemon juice if required. Now mix to a smooth paste. Serve spread thickly on hot toast*. Use for canapés, garnished with tomato wedges and parsley. Spread thinly in sandwiches. 🦋 A very simple recipe that does not involve cooking

SALMON PASTE   ***

Method: Drain a small can of red salmon. Put into a small basin and mash with a fork. Do not remove any skin or bones but mash these as well. Add about 1 teaspoon soft margarine (heaped) and about ½ a teaspoon fresh lemon juice. ⊂⊣ Mix until you have a smooth paste. Season to taste. For a richer paste, for parties, add 2 to 3 teaspoons double cream instead of the margarine. ⊂⊣ Use for canapés and garnish with thin slices of cucumber, lemon and parsley. ⊂⊣ Also makes a good sandwich spread. ⊂⊣

SARDINE PASTE   ***

Method: Use sardines tinned in oil for this. Drain them on kitchen paper and put into a basin. ⊂⊣ Mash with a fork, adding 1 level teaspoon soft margarine and 1 generous teaspoon tomato purée. ⊂⊣ Mix to a smooth paste. Add a few drops wine vinegar or lemon juice and pepper to taste. ⊂⊣ Use for canapés, garnished with chopped hardboiled egg and tomato slices. ⊂⊣ Spread in sandwiches and cover with tomato slices. A very tasty spread, but rather strong in aroma! ⊂⊣

EGG AND WATERCRESS SPREAD   ****

Method: Put peeled hardboiled egg into a basin and chop with a knife. Add 2 teaspoons top of the milk or single cream and mash to a paste with a fork. Finely chop 3 sprigs per egg and mix well into the paste. Season and use as a sandwich filling or for canapés. Garnish with watercress. 🌿 If making a large amount for a party, make in a blender.

* Must be gluten-free/wheat-free

CURRIED EGG SPREAD

***

Method: Mash hardboiled egg to a paste with a knob of soft margarine. Add 3 good pinches curry powder* per egg. ❀ Mix well and add a little salt to taste. ❀ Use as a sandwich filling or for canapés . Top with cucumber slices or tomato, or half a walnut. ❀ If you are not pleased with the colour of the spread add a tiny bit of tomato purée. ❀

MAYONNAISE

***

1 level tablespoon ground rice
8 tablespoons water
2 level tablespoons soya flour
3 tablespoons wine vinegar
8 tablespoons sunflower oil
3 level teaspoons caster sugar
1 level teaspoon salt
1 level teaspoon made mustard*

Method: Put the ground rice into a small saucepan with the water and cook for about 4 minutes while you stir. The mixture should be smooth and thick. ➜ Allow to grow cold. ➜ Press the soya flour with the back of a spoon to get out any lumps. Put into a blender with the rest of the ingredients and blend to a cream. ➜

Variation: Use 1 tablespoon of wine vinegar less and add 1 heaped teaspoon tomato purée. ➜

Store in the fridge for up to a week, in a screw-top jar. Make sure you use a made mustard which does not contain wheat or gluten. (Look for French Mustard). ➜

* Must be gluten-free/wheat-free

127

SALAD DRESSING

***

2 heaped teaspoons made mustard*
2 tablespoons cider or wine vinegar
4 tablespoons sunflower oil
4 grinds of black pepper
¼ teaspoon salt
2 heaped teaspoons soft brown sugar

Method: Put all ingredients into a screw-top jar. Make sure the lid is screwed on tightly and shake vigorously to blend. Shake before serving and store in the fridge.

Variations:
1. Omit the mustard
2. Crush in a small clove of garlic.
3. Add ¼ of a medium sized onion, finely chopped.

CRUDITÉS

*****

For a party allow the amounts that are given for one person (in brackets) multiplied by the number of guests.

Radishes: scrubbed and trimmed (3 or 4 depending on size)
Celery: scrubbed and trimmed and cut into short lengths. If the stalks are large then cut through lengthways as well. (3 pieces)
Carrot: wash and trim, cut into large matchstick shapes (3)
Spring Onion: wash, trim off tough green parts and roots (2)
Cauliflower: use the crisp white curds. Wash well and break or cut into florets. (2)
Lettuce: use just the heart leaves. Wash and pat dry with a clean teatowel. For parties use several varieties of lettuce as available — Cos, Little Gem, Density, Webb's Wonder etc.
Tomato: only use if you can get small fruits (parties). For packed meals any size will do. (2 small or 1 medium)

If serving for a party use a tray or large plates and arrange the vegetables in circles with a bowl of mayonnaise in the centre for use as a dip. Use up the larger lettuce leaves as a cool base.

* Must be gluten-free/wheat-free

If using for a packed lunch make sure the vegetables are all dried well after preparation. Put carefully into a polythene bag, loosely packed. Tie the bag. Mayonnaise (optional) can be packed in a separate container such as a small screw-top jar. (Unless the bag can be kept cool , don't put in any cauliflower). Crudités are easy to eat with the fingers and keep fresher than a salad. Salt can be packed in a screw of paper.

SAVOURY TARTLETS   ***

Method: Use the same pastry as for Jam Tarts but bake blind.
Allow to cool. Make a quantity of White Sauce* using a
richer mixture of ¼ single cream to ¾ milk instead of all milk.
Use as a base for the following flavours. Allow three teaspoons
filling per tartlet.   For flavouring each tartlet allow:—

Prawn: 2 or 3 prawns depending on size/3 drops lemon juice/
3 good pinches chopped parsley/ salt and pepper to taste.
Garnish with lemon slice and parsley sprig.

Chicken: 1 heaped teaspoon finely chopped cold, roast chicken
meat (white and red meat mixed)/ 3 pinches chopped parsley/
salt and pepper to taste. Garnish with parsley sprig.

Ham: 1 heaped teaspoon chopped ham (without breadcrumb
coating). Remove all fat before chopping and use ham that is
not cut too thinly. Season to taste. Garnish with parsley.

Mushroom: Chop mushrooms finely and fry in a little cooking
oil. Drain well and stir into the sauce. Season to taste. Allow
1 button mushroom per tart or ¼ of a medium sized mushroom.
Garnish with parsley or watercress.

If serving hot do not garnish. Heat the tartlets on a baking sheet
in a moderate oven for 10 minutes. Do not leave them in too
long or the fillings will develop a skin and the pastry will be too
dry. Serve on warmed plates.

* Must be gluten-free/wheat-free

129

PASTIES

Shortcrust Pastry — use the Half Recipe from the Section on
   Puddings and Pastries (page 113)
Filling — choose from one of the following

Fish   small can of tuna fish in oil, drained/slice of onion
         finely chopped/1 medium tomato, chopped/ salt and
         freshly ground black pepper to taste
Meat   2 oz lean, minced beef (50 g)/slice of onion, finely
         chopped/ 1 small potato, coarsely grated/ salt and
         freshly ground black pepper to taste/ dash of soy sauce*

Preheat oven: Regulo 7 (220°C or 425°F)
Position: above centre of oven
Baking time: about 20 minutes

Method: Divide the dough into 2 or 3 pieces. Roll out between
sheets of greaseproof. Remove top sheet. Divide the filling equally
between the pieces, as shown. Dampen the edges all the way round.

Lift the greaseproof to help you lap the pastry
over the filling. Press the edges together to seal
and trim neatly with a knife. Lift on to an
ungreased baking sheet with the help of a
spatula. Cut a slit in the top of each one to let
out the steam during cooking. Brush with
beaten egg and bake. Serve hot or cold.

The filling ingredients should be mixed well before use. Not quite
high enough in protein to serve for a main meal but makes a good
snack or supper dish. Ideal for packed lunches too.

SAVOURY CHOUX BUNS

Method: Make as for Profiteroles but omit sugar. When cold
fill with cream cheese into which a little cold milk has been
beaten to make it lighter. Alternatively, fill with any of the
patés and spreads in this section , slices of tomato or chopped
hard boiled egg can be used as well as the fillings to add colour.

* Must be gluten-free/wheat-free

QUICHE

Shortcrust Pastry — use the recipe from the section on Puddings
        and Pastries (page 113)
2 eggs
½ pint milk (300 ml)
4 oz grated cheese (100 g)

Preheat oven: Regulo 7 (220° C or 425° F)
Position: above centre of oven
Baking time: 15 minutes for pastry case and 30 minutes for filling
        on a lower temperature

Method: Make the pastry as recipe directs. Put into an 8 inch
(20 cm) flan dish and press out with the fingers, pushing the dough
up the sides as well. Trim off neatly with a knife and press the
edge slightly over the rim of the dish. ❁ Bake. Remove from oven
and turn down the heat to Regulo 5 (190°C or 375°F). Next
make the filling. Whisk the eggs with the milk. Stir in the cheese
and pour into the pastry case. Put back into the oven to cook the
filling for about half an hour or until the filling has set. ❁ Serve hot
or cold. ❁

Variations: Omit cheese and instead put in 3 cooked rashers streaky
bacon, chopped into pieces. Lay slices of tomato on the top and
a sprinkle of fresh chopped parsley. ❁ ❁ Omit cheese and put
in 4 oz prawns (100 g). ❁❁❁Omit cheese and put in 4 oz
fried mushrooms, chopped small. Sprinkle with fresh chopped
parsley. ❁❁❁ Omit half of the cheese and put in 4 oz fried
sliced onions (100 g). ❁ ❁ ❁

SOUPS

Amounts are given for 1 portion (for a packed meal) or for
12 (for a party). Use a thin soy sauce that does not contain
gluten or wheat such as the ones suggested in the list at the
back of this book.

TOMATO SOUP — inexpensive and always popular   ******

For One: ¼ of a medium onion, peeled and sliced/ small knob
of margarine/ ¼ medium tin tomatoes/¼ pint water (150 ml)/
½ teaspoon soy sauce*/ pinch or two of sugar to taste/ salt
and freshly ground black pepper to taste/ 1 level teaspoon
chopped parsley (fresh)

For Twelve: 3 medium sized onions/ 3 oz (75 g) margarine/
3 medium tins tomatoes/ 3 pints (2000 ml) water/ 1½ tablespoons
soy sauce*/ sugar to taste/ salt and freshly ground pepper to
taste (black)/ 3 level tablespoons chopped parsley (fresh)

Method: Fry the onion in the margarine for 4 or 5 minutes
but do not let it brown. Liquidize with the tomatoes and
some of the water. Put back in the pan and add the rest of
the water and the soy sauce*. Heat to boiling point then
simmer for 4 minutes. Add sugar and seasoning to taste. If
the tomatoes are sweet you will not need any sugar. Just
before serving, sprinkle in the parsley. 🍅🍅🍅

VEGETABLE SOUP   *******

For One: 1 teaspoon thin cooking oil/ ¼ medium onion,
peeled and sliced/ small piece each of prepared carrot,
turnip, parsnip and potato/ 1 sprout/ ¼ pint water (150 ml)
1 scant teaspoon soy sauce*/ salt and freshly ground black
pepper

For Twelve: 3 tablespoons thin cooking oil/ 3 medium
onions, peeled and sliced/ 3 medium carrots, scrubbed and
sliced/ 3 small turnips, scrubbed, trimmed and sliced/
3 small parsnips, scrubbed, trimmed and sliced/ 12 sprouts,
prepared and sliced/ 3 medium potatoes, peeled and sliced/
2½ tablespoons soy sauce*/ salt and freshly ground black
pepper/ about 3 pints water (litres)

132   * Must be gluten-free/wheat-free

Method: Fry the onion in the oil. Add the vegetables and most of the water. Spoon in the soy sauce.* Bring to the boil and simmer with the lid on for about 15 to 20 minutes. Remove from heat. Add the remaining water and liquidize. Return to pan. Season to taste and serve hot. 🍃 Optional — serve with a sprinkle of finely chopped fresh parsley. 🍃

SPLIT PEA SOUP — a very filling soup   * * * * *

For One: 2 oz split peas (50 g)/ 1 small onion, peeled and sliced/ small knob of margarine/ ¼ pint water (150 ml)/ 1 teaspoon soy sauce*/ 2 oz carrot, washed and sliced (50 g)/ salt and freshly ground pepper (black) to taste

For Twelve: 1½ lb split peas (700 g)/ 3 large onions, peeled and sliced/ 3 oz margarine (75 g)/ 3 pints water (2000 ml)/ 3 tablespoons soy sauce*/ 1½ lb carrots (700 g), scrubbed and sliced/ salt and freshly ground black pepper to taste

Method: Wash the split peas in a colander. Leave to soak overnight in a large amount of water . The next day, fry the onion in the margarine for a few minutes. Pour in the water and the soy sauce.* Strain the soaked peas (if necessary) and add to the saucepan with the carrots and a little salt. 🍃 Bring to the boil and simmer gently for 1½ hours, giving a stir every now and then to prevent sticking. If it looks like drying out add more water. Season to taste. If preferred liquidize after cooling. 🍃Reheat to serve and add a sprinkle of finely chopped fresh mint leaves — just one for the single portion (a small one) and about 9 or 10 for the larger amount. 🍃 🍃 🍃

* Must be gluten-free/wheat-free

MUSHROOM SOUP ****

For One: ¼ of a medium onion, peeled and sliced/ 1 teaspoon thin cooking oil/ 1 oz mushrooms, washed and sliced/ about a teacup of water/½ teaspoon soy sauce*/ salt and freshly ground black pepper to taste

For Twelve: 3 medium sized onions, peeled and sliced/ 3 tablespoons thin cooking oil/ ¾ lb mushrooms, washed and sliced (350 g)/ just over 2 pints water (1150 ml)/ 1½ tablespoons soy sauce*/ salt and freshly ground black pepper

Method: Fry the onion in the oil for 3 or 4 minutes but do not let it brown. Liquidize with some of the water, the mushrooms and soy sauce. Bring to the boil with the rest of the water. Simmer for 5 minutes and season to taste.

PARTIES

Here are some suggestions for different types of parties. Use as a basic guide for the amounts of food people will probably eat and also the type of food that is suitable.

Adult's Buffet Supper or Lunch

Allow for each person:—
1. 1 helping crudités
2. 2 slices cold meat — chicken, ham (without breadcrumb coating), beef etc.
3. 1 portion of a savoury pastry dish or 3 savoury tartlets (quiche, pasty or pie)
4. 1 portion of mixed salad
5. hot soup, 1 portion
6. fresh fruit or fruit salad (fresh)

* Must be gluten-free/wheat-free

Cocktail Party

Allow for each person:—

1. 3 canapés
2. 2 savoury choux buns*
3. 6 cocktail biscuits or cheese nibbles or similar
4. small portion nuts — peanuts or toasted almonds
5. 2 cocktail onions on sticks
6. 2 cocktail gherkins on sticks
7. few plain potato crisps
8. 2 cocktail sticks with a cube of pineapple and a cube
   of cheddar cheese

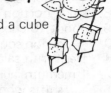

Childrens' Tea Party — (ages 4 to 7)

Allow for each child:—

1. 1 portion fruit jelly
2. 1 slice Victoria Sponge or similar
3. 6 cheese nibbles
4. small portion plain crisps
5. slice celebration cake
6. 2 slices special bread* and Marmite
7. 2 slices special toast*and honey
8. 1 iced bun or 2 novelty biscuits
9. glass milk or homemade lemonade

Also allow special bread and butter but don't make it until
you are sure they are going to eat it. i.e. Don't waste it.

Childrens' High Tea/Early Supper — for ages 7 and up

Allow for each child:—

1. 2 Hamburgers * or fish cakes* with Heinz Baked Beans
2. 2 slices special bread and butter
3. Fruit Salad and ice cream*
4. 1 slice celebration cake
5. generous portion plain crisps
6. portion cheese nibbles or similar
7. 1 large glass (or more) of Coca-cola, milk or lemonade

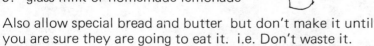

* Must be gluten-free/wheat-free

135

Teenagers' Party

Allow for each teenager:—

1. 1 generous portion quiche or pizza
2. 1 slice celebration cake
3. 4 canapés, assorted
5. generous portion plain cheese and 3 special biscuits
      for cheese such as crispbreads*
6. 1 slice tart du jour and cream or 2 éclairs
7. 1 portion crudités
8. small portion nuts
9. about 10 cheese nibbles*
10. 1 portion soup*
11. fresh fruit salad or fruit in season
12. 1 medium jacket potato or potato chips (served in
       shifts when ready)

PACKED MEALS

Try to balance the packed meal as you would one at home. Protein, vegetables and fruit and not too much carbohydrate. Pack different items separately in containers, foil or polythene bags. Then pack everything into one large container. Wide-necked vacuum flasks can be bought at good ironmongers.

Large Packed Lunch

1. Thermos of hot soup*
2. Protein food such as cold meat, hardboiled eggs, quiche,*
      pasty,* liver paté,* tin of salmon or sardines or baked
      beans*
3. Crudités or salad with dressing in a separate container
4. Fruit or a fruit jelly
5. Slice of cake* or cheese and crispbread*
6. Thermos of hot tea or coffee with dried milk in a separate
      container

(Don't forget tin-opener, salt, plate and cutlery)

* Must be gluten-free/wheat-free

Packed Hot Meal

Use 2 wide-necked vacuum flasks.
1. Hot rice, slightly undercooked
2. Hot beef casserole* or curry* slightly undercooked
3. Fruit salad in a screwtop jar or 2 pieces fresh fruit
4. Hot tea or coffee with dried milk in a separate container
(Don't forget plate, cutlery, salt.)

GREEN SALADS   (With minimum of dressing) *****

Method: Use any combination of the following prepared greens and dress just before serving with an oil/vinegar dressing. Season to taste with salt and freshly ground black pepper.

1. Lettuce — Little Gem, Cos, Flat, Webb's Wonder, Salad Bowl etc. Tear into small pieces and use as a base for the salad.
2. Watercress, torn into sprigs.
3. Cress, cut off near the roots.
4. Sprouts, shredded finely.
5. Young broccoli or spinach leaves, torn into small pieces.
6. Cold cooked peas or green beans.
7. Small leaves of curly kale, cut into pieces.
8. Tender leaves of green cabbage, shredded.
9. Sliced cucumber.

RED SALADS   *****

Method: Use any combination of the following prepared vegetables. Dress just before serving with an oil/vinegar dressing. Season to taste with salt and freshly ground black pepper.

1. Red pepper, chopped small
2. Red cabbage, shredded finely.
3. Carrot, finely grated.
4. Tomato, sliced small.
5. Raw, grated beetroot.

* Must be gluten-free/wheat-free

MIXED SALADS

The following salads are in amounts for one person. They should be dressed with the minimum amount of dressing — just enough to make the salad moist.

1. Mix the following in a bowl. Season to taste and add ½ teaspoon lemon juice and 1 teaspoon oil. **1 tender leaf of curly kale, 1 heaped teaspoon raisins, ½ medium carrot, grated, 2 heaped tablespoons coarsely grated cauliflower.**

2. Mix the following in a bowl with 2 teaspoons oil/vinegar dressing and seasoning to taste. **1 portion crisp cabbage , finely shredded, 1 teaspoon sultanas (heaped), ½ an eating apple, grated, 1 heaped teaspoon finely chopped onion, 1 heaped tablespoon grated carrot.**

3. Mix the following in a bowl. Season to taste and add 2 teaspoons oil/vinegar dressing. **2 medium mushrooms, chopped, 4 lettuce leaves torn into pieces, ½ packet cress cut up with scissors, eating apple, grated (about ¼), ¼ small parsnip, grated, sprinkle of sugar.**

4. Mix the following in a bowl with seasoning to taste and oil/vinegar dressing. **2 medium tomatoes, chopped, ½ stalk celery, chopped, piece of green pepper, chopped, 1 medium mushroom sliced, 1 portion watercress, torn into sprigs, few raisins or cold, cooked peas.**

Any of these four salads can be mixed with a cup of cold, cooked rice to make it more substantial, or, better still, served with a potato baked in its jacket. The easiest way to cook these is to put a metal meat skewer through the middle of each large one to make sure it cooks in the middle. An hour at Regulo 7 (220° C or 425° F), top shelf will be ample. Remember to prick the skins before baking. Serve with a cut down the middle and a knob of butter or margarine melting in the centre. *****

Extras

MUESLI   *****

Method: Start with a base (1 level tablespoon) of Trufree or Jubilee Crispbran, or, 1 heaped tablespoon cooked rice. Add a sliced banana, half an eating apple, coarsely grated and a little honey or brown sugar. Top with a sprinkle of dried fruit such as chopped apricots, raisins or sultanas and another sprinkle of sunflower and sesame seeds. Pour on fruit juice or milk and you have a good start to the day or a snack for supper. The Crispbran is made from soya bran toasted with fructose and is a good source of fibre. Any fresh fruits in season will add variety. Almonds and walnuts can be added too.

RICE PORRIDGE — one smallish helping   ***

¼ pint milk (150 ml)
1 heaped tablespoon ground rice
few raisins or sultanas
small knob of margarine
1 heaped teaspoon sugar
2 heaped teaspoons ground almonds

Method: Put the milk and rice into a saucepan and mix until smooth. Add the fruit and margarine and heat to boiling. Cook while you stir for 3 to 4 minutes until the porridge thickens. Add the sugar and ground almonds. Mix and serve right away. Use for breakfast as it is. Serve with stewed fruit as a pudding but leave out the dried fruit.

139

REAL CUSTARD

***

1 large egg
2 tablespoons caster sugar
few drops vanilla flavouring
½ pint milk (275 ml)

Method: Put the egg and sugar into a basin and mix well. Heat the milk but don't let it get to boiling point. Pour it on to the egg/sugar while you whisk. Put it back into the milk pan and gradually heat while you stir. Again, don't let it boil. When it has thickened enough to coat the spoon take it off the heat and serve, after adding the vanilla flavouring to taste. Stir in well. 🦋

MINCEMEAT

****

2 oz each of raisins, brown sugar, melted margarine and
    chopped almonds (50 g)
3 oz each of sultanas and currants (75 g)
1 medium, grated eating apple
½ teaspoon each of allspice, cinnamon and nutmeg
grated rind of 1 orange
orange juice or brandy to moisten

Method: Put all ingredients into a bowl except the juice or brandy. Mix well, then moisten with orange juice or brandy. Put into jars, cover and store in the fridge. Will keep for several weeks. 🦋🦋 Use for mincepies, tarts and to stuff baked apples.

Does not contain suet like the commercial kinds of mincemeat, which may contain wheat/gluten. 🦋 Very easy to make. 🦋

SAGE AND ONION STUFFING

***

2 large onions, peeled
1 teacup special breadcrumbs*
1 oz margarine
1 level teaspoon dried sage
1 egg
salt and freshly ground black pepper to taste

Method: Put the onions into a saucepan with about ½ pint water (300 ml) and bring to the boil. Simmer steadily for about 20 minutes to partly cook the onion. Remove from the water and put on a chopping board. Chop into small pieces and put into a basin with the rest of the ingredients. Mix well and use for stuffing poultry. Any of the Trufree/Jubilee breads will do for the breadcrumbs.

PARSLEY AND THYME STUFFING

***

1 large onion
2 oz margarine (50 g)
2 level tablespoons chopped parsley (fresh)
milk to moisten
grated rind of ½ lemon
½ teaspoon (level) dried thyme
salt and pepper to taste

Method: Peel and chop the onion then fry in the margarine until transparent. Put the onion into a bowl with all other ingredients and mix well with a fork. Use enough milk to make the stuffing sticky. Use for stuffing meat or fish.

* Must be gluten-free/wheat-free

141

BREAD SAUCE

1 teacup special breadcrumbs*
1 oz margarine (25 g)
1 small onion
½ pint milk (300 ml)
2 or 3 cloves
salt and pepper to taste

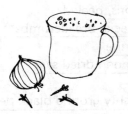

Method: Peel the onion and stick the cloves firmly into it. Put it
into the milk with the other ingredients and bring the milk gently
to the boil. Remove from heat and leave to stand in a warm place.
When you want to serve it, remove the onion and discard. Heat
the sauce gently while you beat with a wooden spoon. Serve in
a sauceboat with a spoon. Serve with roast chicken. Bread made
with   Trufree/Jubilee flours no. 1 or No. 4 are best for the
bread to make the crumbs. ✿

GRAVY

**

Method: Mix 1 heaped teaspoon maize flour or cornflour* with 2
tablespoons water. Add 2 teaspoons soy sauce*. Pour into strainings
from vegetables, mix well and bring to the boil.   Simmer while you
stir for a couple of minutes. ✿ If there are any meat juices from the
grill pan or roasting tin, so much the better. Add these after draining
off all the fat. Sometimes it is easier to make the gravy in the grill
pan or roasting tin instead of a saucepan. ✿

An alternative way to make gravy for a roast dinner is to first strain
off all fat from the roasting tin. Sprinkle in a tablespoon of Trufree
or Jubilee No.6 plain flour and rub into the meat juices with a wooden
spoon. Gradually add the strainings from the vegetables while you
heat and stir to a rich gravy. Add a dash of soy sauce* if you wish.
This type of gravy will be acceptable to the whole family. ✿

* Must be gluten-free/wheat-free

WHITE SAUCE

***

1 oz butter or margarine (25 g)
1 oz Trufree or Jubilee No. 6 Plain flour (25 g)
½ pint milk (300 ml)

Method: Heat the butter or margarine gently in a small saucepan.
Remove from heat and stir in the flour. Return to the heat and
cook for a minute while stirring. Remove from the heat again and
gradually blend in the cold milk, beating well to get out any lumps.
When you have put in all the milk and the mixture is smooth, put
back on the heat and bring to the boil. Cook while stirring for
another couple of minutes. Season to taste.

CHEESE SAUCE

**

Method: Make the White Sauce recipe. Stir in 3 to 4 oz (75 to 100 g)
of finely grated cheese such as cheddar. Also add 1 level teaspoon
French Mustard*. Stir both in well until the cheese has melted.
Use on cooked cauliflower to make Cauliflower Cheese or to pour
over Canelloni*.

PARSLEY SAUCE

****

Method: Make the White Sauce recipe. Stir in 2 heaped teaspoons
fresh parsley, finely chopped. Serve with fish or use as a base for
savoury tartlets with prawns.

HOLLANDAISE SAUCE

***

Method: Make White Sauce recipe. Remove from heat and allow to
cool a little. Whisk in 1 egg and 2 teaspoons fresh lemon juice.
Put back on the heat and cook for a few more minutes over a very
gentle heat. Serve with fish. ☺

ONION SAUCE

****

Method: Peel and boil 3 medium onions. Make the White Sauce
recipe. Chop the onions and add to the sauce. Mix in well and serve
hot with lamb.

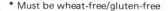

* Must be wheat-free/gluten-free

YORKSHIRE PUDDING 1 — makes 12 small or 1 large

4 oz Trufree or Jubilee flour No. 7 S.R.   (100 g)

3 pinches salt

1 egg

1 tablespoon cooking oil

½ pint milk (300 ml)

oil for the baking tin(s)

Preheat oven: Regulo 9 (245°C or 475°F)
Position: top shelf
Baking time: 5 minutes + 30 minutes at a lower heat

Method: Put the flour, salt and tablespoon of oil into a bowl.
Mix and make a well in the centre. ❋ Break the egg into it and
stir into the mix. ❋ Gradually add the milk and stir in, beating
as soon as you are able, to form a milky batter. ❋   Heat 2 to 3
tablespoons oil in a baking tin or 12 patty tins. Pour or spoon in
the batter. ❋ Bake for 5 minutes and then turn down the heat to
Regulo 7 (220°C or 425°F) for the remaining baking time. Serve
immediately with roast beef etc. ❋

These are indistinguishable from those made with wheat flour so
you can serve them to the whole family. If you feel this type is
too greasy try the choux pastry ones in the following recipe. ❋

YORKSHIRE PUDDING 2 — makes 12 small

4 oz Trufree or Jubilee No. 7 S.R. flour (100 g)

¼ pint water (150 ml)

1 oz margarine (25 g)

4 teaspoons cooking oil

2 eggs, beaten

Preheat oven : Regulo 6 (200°C or 400°F)
Position: centre of oven
Baking time: 20 minutes

Method: Put the water, margarine and oil into a saucepan and heat gently until the margarine has melted. Add the flour and stir well over a medium heat to cook the mixture. Continue until it forms one ball. Remove from heat and gradually beat in the egg.❋ Grease and flour a baking sheet. ❋ Use a teaspoon to put 12 dollops of the dough on to it, leaving plenty of space around each one. ❋ Bake until golden, well risen and crisp. Serve hot with roast beef etc. ❋

* * * * *

FISH CAKES — makes 6 generous cakes

8 oz cod, haddock or coley (225 g)
juice of ½ a lemon
8 oz cold mashed potato (225 g)
1 oz margarine (25 g)
1 tablespoon chopped, fresh parsley
salt and pepper
oil for frying

Method: Poach fish in water for a few minutes.   Strain and remove any bones. ⊲ Add all other ingredients and mix well with a fork until the fish is evenly distributed, in small pieces. ⊲ Form into round cakes with the hands.   Fry in shallow oil for about 3 to 4 minutes on each side. ⊲ Can be stored overnight in the fridge. Makes a good breakfast with special bread and butter and tomato sauce*or grilled tomatoes.   Allow extra cooking time if the fish-cakes are cooked straight from the fridge. ⊲

Variations: Use a small tin of salmon instead of the fresh fish. Do not bother to remove bones as they will be soft enough to eat. ⊲

Dip the fishcakes in beaten egg before frying. ⊲

Dip the fishcakes in beaten egg and then roll in special breadcrumbs. Fry in the usual way. ⊲

Mix 2 heaped teaspoons tomato purée into the mashed potato for amazingly coloured fishcakes. Popular novelty for children. ⊲

* Must be gluten-free/wheat-free

145

FISH FINGERS

****

Method: Cut fresh fillets of cod or haddock (thick) into neat finger shapes. Dip in beaten egg and roll in special breadcrumbs*. Fry in hot oil, turning once. Allow about 4 to 5 minutes each side so that they are cooked right through. Serve immediately. Any of the Trufree/Jubilee special breads will do for the breadcrumbs.

STEAK AND MUSHROOM PIE — 2 servings

***

Filling:

4 oz lean stewing beef (100 g)

2 medium mushrooms

1 level tablespoon maize flour or cornflour*

2 teaspoons soy sauce*

1 small onion, sliced

2 teaspoons oil

water

salt and freshly ground black pepper to taste

Method: Fry the onion in the oil. Trim the steak and cut into smallish pieces. Roll the meat in the maize flour and add to the onion. Stir while you fry, to seal the meat. Pour in enough water to cover and the soy sauce. Put in the mushrooms, chopped. Season and bring to the boil. Simmer gently for about 45 minutes or put in the oven at Regulo 6 (200°C or 400°F) and cook as a casserole. If it starts to get dry, put in a little more water. When ready, drain and keep the juice to use as gravy.

Pastry:

half recipe of Shortcrust Pastry from Puddings and Pastries Section

Preheat oven: Regulo 7 (220°C or 425°F)
Position: above centre of oven
Baking time: about 20 minutes

146   *Must be gluten-free/wheat-free

Method: Line a small oval pie-dish with the pastry, leaving enough dough to make the lid. Press out with the fingers. Roll out the lid between 2 sheets of greaseproof paper. 🐌 Put in the cooked filling and dampen the edges of the pastry. Remove the top sheet of paper and turn the pastry upsidedown over the pie. Remove paper and trim with a knife. Press edges together to seal and cut a slit in the top to let out the steam during baking. Brush with beaten egg and bake. Serve hot or cold, with hot vegetables and gravy or with salad and hot potatoes. If serving hot use the rest of the juice for gravy.

HAMBURGERS — makes 4 generous ones   ***

8 oz lean, minced beef (225 g)
1 slice special bread* made into crumbs
1 egg, beaten
salt and freshly ground black pepper to taste
1 teaspoon soy sauce*
1 small onion, peeled and finely chopped
oil for frying
ground rice

Method: Put all ingredients except the last 2 into a bowl and mix well with a fork. 🐌 Shape by hand into flat round cakes. Dip into ground rice to form a thin coating. 🐌 Fry in shallow hot oil for 3 or 4 minutes. Turn carefully and fry on the other side for another 3 or 4 minutes. 🌿🐌 Serve as a hot snack between 2 slices of special bread* and Tomato Sauce* or, as part of a main meal with potatoes and vegetables. (Allow 2 per person). 🌿🐌
🐌 These Hamburgers can be made in advance and kept in the fridge for a few hours before frying. Stack on a plate with small sheets of greaseproof between them.   Any of the Trufree or Jubilee breads will do for the breadcrumbs. 🌿🐌

* Must be gluten-free/wheat-free

PASTA — makes 10 oz of dough   ****

8 oz Trufree or Jubilee No. 4 flour (225 g)

2 tablespoons oil such as sunflower oil

3 tablespoons cold water

3 pinches salt

1 egg, beaten

Method: Put the flour and salt into a bowl and mix. Add the
2 tablespoons oil and rub in.✿ Put in the egg and mix. Lastly,
add the water and mix again to a sticky paste. Knead, adding
a small quantity of extra flour if you need to. Take out of the
bowl and knead on a cool worktop until smooth. Divide the
dough into 4 portions. Roll out each portion on a floured*
surface, as thin as you can.✿ Cut into strips about ¼ inch wide
(4 mm) and drop into boiling salted water (plenty). Cook
steadily for about 12 minutes and taste to see if it is cooked. ✿
It should be 'al dente', that is, it should be tender but firm.
Drain in a colander and serve with Bolognese Sauce*(see Extras
Section) and a sprinkling of Parmesan cheese. Cooked pasta
will keep overnight in the fridge and can be warmed up, in a sauce*
the following day. ✿ The dough can also be rolled out to make
flat sheets of pasta for Canelloni. Cut into 3 x 4 inch rectangles
(7.5 x 10 cm). Drop into boiling, salted water and cook for
about 12 minutes.

CANELLONI   ****

Method: Cook the pasta rectangles and drain. Place on a clean
tea towel and pat dry. Spread as shown in the diagram, with
Bolognese Sauce on its own or mixed with cooked chopped
spinach. Roll up and place in a greased , shallow ovenproof dish.
Cover with cheese sauce* (see recipe in Extras Section) and bake
in a preheated oven at Regulo 6 (200 C°or 400°F) for about 20
minutes, by which time it will be bubbling. (Bake on a shelf
above the centre of the oven.) Serve hot with a green side-salad.✿

148   * Must be gluten-free/wheat-free

SAVOURY ROLLS

****

Shortcrust Pastry dough — half recipe makes 6 rolls — see section
on Puddings and Pastries for recipe
filling — use one of the following
beaten egg for glaze

Cheese and Onion

½ a small onion, chopped
2 oz grated cheese (50 g)
½ an eating apple, coarsely grated
salt and freshly ground black pepper to taste
½ a beaten egg

Meat

2 oz fresh minced, lean, beef, veal or pork (50 g)
1 small mushroom, chopped
1 small potato, peeled and coarsely grated
½ a beaten egg
salt and freshly ground black pepper to taste

Preheat oven: Regulo 7 (220°C or 425°F)
Position: above centre of oven
Baking time: about 20 minutes

Method: Roll out the pastry between 2 sheets of greaseproof paper.
Remove top sheet. Cut into rectangles and spoon on filling as shown.
 Brush pastry edges with water. Use the greaseproof paper to
help you lap the pastry over the filling. Press edges together to seal.
Slash the tops with a knife as shown. Brush with beaten egg and
bake. Serve hot or cold. 🥬 If you find it easier, make 1 long roll
on the greaseproof paper and cut into smaller ones.

As ordinary sausage rolls and sausagemeat are made with ordinary
bread as a filler, these savoury rolls will fill the gap. 🥬🥬🥬

Filling ingredients should be mixed together in a small basin.

149

BOLOGNESE SAUCE — 2 servings

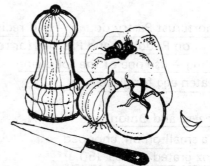

½ medium onion
2 teaspoons oil
½ clove garlic
2 medium sized mushrooms
2 oz lean, minced beef (50 g)
small piece green pepper
small tin tomatoes
2 teaspoons soy sauce*
salt and freshly ground black pepper to taste

Method: Peel and chop the onion and fry in the oil until transparent. Put in the beef and fry lightly until it turns to a pinkish-brown colour. Add the mushrooms, chopped pepper and the tomatoes. 🍃 🍃 Bring to the boil and simmer for about 8 to 10 minutes, giving it a stir from time to time. Add the soy sauce*, crush in the garlic and season to taste. Serve hot on special pasta* (see recipe in this section) with a sprinkle of Parmesan cheese on top. Can be stored overnight in the fridge, in a sealed container. 🍃 Reheat the following day in a saucepan. 🍃

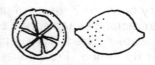

*

LEMONADE

Method: Wash a lemon and cut into slices. ✂ Put into a jug and pour over about 3 teacups boiling water. Sprinkle in a tablespoon of sugar. Leave to steep for about 12 hours. Strain and discard the lemon pieces. ✂ Use instead of orange squash, diluted with water. Serve with ice cubes and a slice of fresh lemon. A very refreshing and simple to make drink. One lemon makes enough to dilute into about 10 drinks. ✂ Store in the fridge and use up within a few days. ✂

* Must be gluten-free/wheat-free

USEFUL INFORMATION

SPECIAL INGREDIENTS
Wherever a star appears next to an ingredient * in this book it indicates that care must be taken to choose a gluten-free/wheat-free brand. However, manufacturers can change their formulas at any time, so please check all ingredients labelling carefully before using such products.

STOCK
The authour recommends Vecon Vegetable Stock as suitable for gluten-free/wheat-free cooking. Available from health stores.

YEAST
The yeast supplied free with Trufree/Jubilee Flours is just PURE yeast without any additives. Like the flours it is milk and lactose free.

RECIPE ERRORS
Apologies for the following slight errors in this book.
PIZZA page 14 — add ½ teaspoon each of cream of tartar and bicarbonate of soda to the flour.

VANILLA CREAMS page 30 — add the flavouring after the egg.
GINGER NUTS page 45 — add 2 oz (50 g) sugar to the ingredients.
BUTTER BISCUITS page 51 — heat the sugar with the butter.
JAM DOUGHNUTS page 90 — add the sugar with the flour.
BAKEWELL TART page 115 — add the ground almonds with the breadcrumbs.

FREEZING
Foods cooked with Trufree/Jubilee Flours can be frozen as for ordinary food. However, freezing foods does nothing to improve them.

CONTAMINATION
People on just wheat-free diets should also avoid rye, barley and oats as these are traditionally processed and packed in the same place as wheat flours, making contamination a certainty.

GLUTEN-FREE/WHEAT-FREE
This list has been compiled from products that contain gluten and/or wheat. If you see anyone of these in an ingredients list, then it may not be suitable for use in gluten-free/wheat-free cooking. Those with a star are definitely unsuitable. Those without a star are questionable.

* Wholewheat or wholegrain
* Wheat and wheat flour
* Wheat starch
* Wheat protein
* Rye and rye flour
* Barley and barley flour
* Barley meal or pearl barley
* Oats, oatmeal, oat flour
* Oat bran, oat germ
* Durum wheat

Food starch
* Special gluten-free food starch
   (usually wheat starch)
* Rusk
* Wheat germ
* Wheat bran or bran
* Flour
Starch
Thickening
* Semolina

The Gluten-free Symbol

This symbol does not mean that products which carry it are wheat-free. It indicates that they were prepared from either naturally gluten-free flours (rarely) or more likely, with gluten-containing flours which have been chemically processed to remove as much of the gluten as possible (never all as this is a scientific impossibility).

The Wheat-free Symbol

Look for a new sign which indicates wheat-free, based on a letter W crossed through with a stalk of wheat. This should be appearing in the latter part of 1982 on some products as a guide.

AVAILABILITY OF SPECIAL FLOURS AND INGREDIENTS

Some Health Food Stores stock items such as Jubilee Flours, Rice Bran, Split Pea Flour and other basic ingredients. Boots Chemists (most branches) stock Trufree Flours or can order them. There is an increasing trend for the small independent baker to stock Trufree/Jubilee Flours and baked goods using these new flours. In theory, any Chemist should be able to supply Trufree Flours, but many are wary of small orders. The Trufree and Jubilee full range of flours can be obtained by mail order both in the UK and abroad. If you would like details please write to Dept BB, Trufree Foods, Larkhall Laboratories, 225 Putney Bridge Road, London, SW15 2PY, England, Tel. 01-870-0971.

Prescriptions for Trufree flours may only be obtained at Chemists, not Health Food Stores, Bakers or by mail order.

Index

Trufree Vitamins and Minerals — specially formulated for exclusion dieters who cannot take ordinary vitamin and mineral tablets. Made without gluten, wheat, grain, egg, lactose, milk and gliadin. They are especially suitable for coeliacs and gluten and wheat allergics.

Trufree Vitamins and Minerals are obtainable at Chemists and some Health Stores. In case of difficulty please write to Trufree Foods Dept BBB, Larkhall Laboratories, 225 Putney Bridge Road, London SW15 2PY. Also available from this address by mail — gluten-free and wheat-free special ingredients and Trufree & Jubilee Flours. Details available on request.

SAFETY IN THE KITCHEN

Be especially careful when frying in deep fat. Never fill the pan more than ½ full and don't leave it unattended with heat underneath it. If a pan does catch fire, switch off the heat and cover the pan with a damp cloth to smother the flame. Don't take off the cloth until the pan is cool or it may burst into flames again. Don't throw water on to it or attempt to carry it while alight. Most of the cases of severe burns are caused by this.

Tea-cloths or washing drying over the cooker — dangerous! Keep electric flex away from the cooker. Don't let your saucepan handles face outwards or over a lighted burner. Keep matches away from children.

MILK-FREE DIETS

All the flours used in this book are free of milk and lactose. Jubilee and Trufree flours are formulated specially for those who are on a milk-free diet as well as a gluten-free/wheat-free one.

To use the recipes for a milk-free diet:—

1. Avoid all margarines except TOMOR (Kosher, milk-free margarine)
2. Avoid butter and use TOMOR instead.
3. Use water instead of milk.
4. If milk forms a major part of the recipe such as in custard tart, then avoid altogether.
5. Do not use cream.
6. Avoid recipes which have cheese in them.

You will find that most of the recipes in this book can be used if you bear in mind these six points. There are only a handful which cannot be used at all, such as custard tart, cheese scones, cheesecake, cheese wafers etc.

Crumpet Rings — These can be bought at good kitchen shops. If you have difficulty in obtaining them here is the address of a shop that will send them by post:— David Mellor, 4 Sloane Square, London SW1 8EE, Tel. 01-730-4259.